# Quick & Easy
# Indoor Topiary

# Quick & Easy
# Indoor Topiary

*Crafting and Decorating with Nature*

## CHRIS JONES

Storey Books
Schoolhouse Road
Pownal, Vermont 05261

*The mission of Storey Communications is to serve our customers by publishing practical information that encourages personal independence in harmony with the environment.*

United States edition published in 1998 by Storey Books, Schoolhouse Road, Pownal, Vermont 05261.

Project Editor  *Rebecca Moy*
Art Editor  *Michelle Stamp*
Designer  *Karin Skånberg*
Copy Editor  *Gwen Rigby*
Photographer  *Jon Bouchier*
Illustrators  *Ian Mitchell and Karin Skånberg*
Art Director  Moira Clinch
Storey Books Editors  *Deborah Balmuth and Robin Catalano*

Copyright © Quarto Inc. 1998

This book was designed and produced by
*Quarto Publishing plc, 6 Blundell Street, London N7 9BH*

Manufactured in Singapore by Bright Arts Pte Ltd.
Printed in China by Leefung-Asco Printers Ltd.

ISBN 1-58017-055-2

Library of Congress Cataloging-in-Publication Data

Jones, Chris. 1961-
Quick and easy indoor topiary:
crafting and decorating with nature/Chris Jones.
p. cm.
Includes index.
ISBN 1-58017-055-2 (pb :alk. paper)
1. Topiary work. 2. Container gardening. 3. Indoor gardening. 4. Nature craft.  I. Title.
SB463.J65  1998         98-3816
715'.1--dc21           CIP

19 95

# CONTENTS

## INTRODUCTION 8
## MATERIALS & EQUIPMENT 10

## CUBES & SQUARES 26

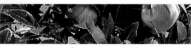

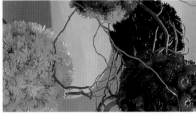

# INTRODUCTION

Topiary is the term applied to the growing and shaping of plants. Traditionally, topiarists have used trees and hedging, such as Buxus *(boxwood)* and Taxus *(yew)*, to make grand displays in large ornamental gardens. These plants have densely-packed foliage that grows quickly and produces strong, sharp shapes, and, being evergreen, they look good all year round. The most common traditional topiaries are geometrically shaped, but designs such as animals and figures can also be seen. Indoor topiary evolved in the nineteenth century, when gardeners began to produce smaller sculptures that could be brought inside, and they developed the more elaborate frames that have become the basis for many of today's topiaries. In this book we show you how easy it is to practice indoor topiary and how to develop the skills you will need to create your own indoor sculpture. We also look at ways of making long-lasting displays from dried and preserved spices, flowers, and leaves.

The pictures (left) show details of aromatic rosemary clipped into cubes; a moss ball and climber topiary; everlasting fruits piled in a glass container to make a fantastic pyramid; and grouped displays of pot-grown cacti, narcissi, and varied miniature topiaries.

The projects range from table-top to floor-standing displays. Step-by-step instructions will help you make the projects and encourage you to create your own beautiful designs.

# MATERIALS & EQUIPMENT

When tackling topiary, the main thing to remember is to choose materials suitable for the type of sculpture you want to create and for the place it will be kept. The mechanics—the frame, container and so on—provide the non-plant backbone of the design, and it is important to get these correct. Prefabricated frames can be bought or you can construct your own, following the instructions given here. All kinds of containers can be used, and often the simpler ones make the topiary look the most stunning. Other materials include florist foam, which can be sculpted and then covered with various materials; sphagnum moss for filling frames; wooden poles for support; potting soil; florist wire; pruning shears; and glue. We also show you how to form the base of some of the designs from chicken wire. The size, maturity and characteristics of the plants are all important, so we suggest the plants most suitable for each project and give alternatives, and we give tips on aftercare to enable you to enjoy your designs to the fullest.

The pictures (left) illustrate this chapter and show details of containers to suit your sculptures; repotting a small bay tree; different-shaped wire frames over which to train plants; and inserting lavender bunches into a florist foam block.

# Choosing a Container

The type of container used for each project in this book is only a suggestion; the most important thing is to choose a container that is suitable for the individual sculpture.

If you are planting living plants, make sure that the drainage is sufficient to prevent the plant becoming waterlogged, and that the container is big enough to allow root growth—especially with shrubs. Make sure the container can stand up to the conditions if the topiary is to be placed outdoors at any time; you can use an otherwise unsuitable decorative container to hide a less attractive functional one. The best containers for plants are made from terracotta, unglazed pottery, and stoneware, since they are porous, but glassware can also be used for shorter periods. Treat metal containers to prevent rusting, and varnish or paint wood to stop moisture from rotting it.

Finding a container for a dried or preserved display is much simpler. The base should be heavy enough to prevent a tall or heavy topiary from toppling over. If in any doubt, set the structure in plaster and add stones for extra weight. Consider where the topiary display will be placed, once in its container a sculpture can be quite heavy; if it will have to be moved often, use a lighter container.

### GLASSWARE
Clean and light-looking, glass is ideal for contemporary arrangements, but you need to hide the mechanics.

### NATURAL
Wooden and basketware containers will give a spontaneous, "earthy" look to your displays.

### INDUSTRIAL
These types of container are very popular for creating topiary with a modern, minimalist feel.

## TERRACOTTA

Although they are usually simple, there is such a huge variety of sizes and shapes that basic terracotta pots are invaluable.

## METALWORK

Traditional topiary is enhanced by leaden urns, while modern designs are well suited to steel and galvanized iron.

## WIREWORK

Decorative wire outer containers can transform a plain inner container.

## COLOR-GLAZED

Pots such as these are available in a multitude of colors and finishes; they are suitable for both living and preserved or dried displays.

## GARDEN CONTAINERS

Although mainly for outdoor use, larger pots may be used inside for a large topiary, particularly if it needs to spend time outdoors.

# Making Frames

Many types of frames are available from garden suppliers. Frames can, however, be quite expensive, and once you have mastered the basic steps you can create your own very easily.

The two main types of frames are two-dimensional and three-dimensional, and are made from a variety of materials. All are suitable for interior use. Traditionally, frames were made from wood, which looks attractive but tends to rot and discolor. Most frames are now made from steel, which can be plastic-coated to prevent rust; copper-coated steel and even antiqued, galvanized wire are available.

Here we show you some simple techniques to make your own frames from cutting, bending, and securing the wire to constructing more ambitious projects. You do not need expensive or specialized tools and materials to create these frames, nor do you have to be artistic because they can be created from the simplest shapes.

## Rigid Wire Frames

You can buy steel wire in several different gauges. Choose the gauge that will support your topiary yet be easy to bend and shape. The higher the gauge number, the thinner the wire—10/12 was used for most of our frames. A thinner copper, or florist, wire is also needed to bind the shapes together. Florist binding tape can be used over the joints to prevent any wire from scratching your hands.

## Chicken Wire Frames

When you have made your base frame, you can cover it with chicken wire, then fill the frame with sphagnum moss to produce a solid base. It comes in several different gauges and hole sizes and for these projects 1/1 is recommended. It is not expensive to buy and very easy to work with.

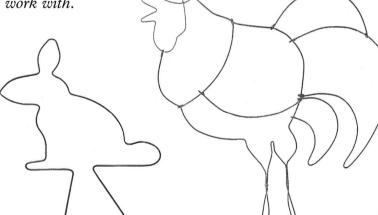

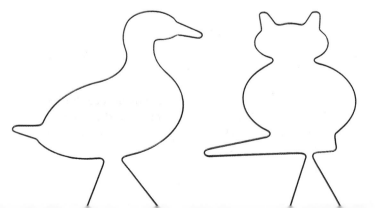

# RIGID WIRE TECHNIQUES

*The first techniques to master are those of bending wire into a support in the shape you want your topiary to take, and then securing and fastening off safely. It will take only a short while to become proficient.*

### BENDING BY HAND

The easiest way to create shapes is by bending the wire. This can be done by hand or with the aid of pliers.

### SECURING

Thinner binding wire is used for this. Wind the wire around several times, and twist the ends together. Cover the joint with florist binding tape.

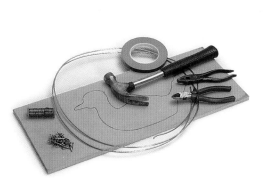

### YOU WILL NEED

- Rigid steel wire
- Hammer and nails
- Board
- Wire cutters
- Pliers
- Binding wire
- Florist binding tape

### BENDING AROUND A CONTAINER

To create soft curves you can use a pot or similar container to bend the wire around.

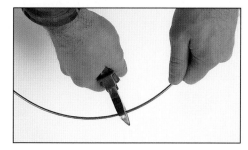

### CUTTING

Using wire cutters, first score the wire, then cut it through. You may find bending the wire slightly at the cutting point will help. Be careful when cutting the wire, since it will produce very sharp edges.

# TWO-DIMENSIONAL DUCK FRAME

*You can make many different designs, from simple geometric shapes to quite complex animal and bird designs, but remember that your chosen shape should have a strong, easily recognizable outline.*

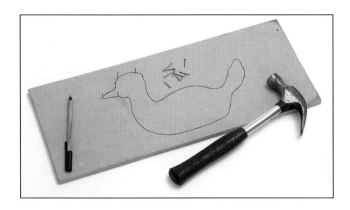

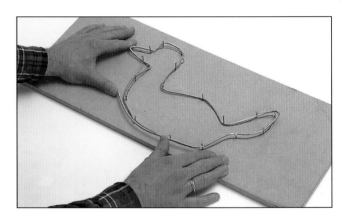

## STEP 3

Continue bending the wire until the two ends meet. Cut off any excess.

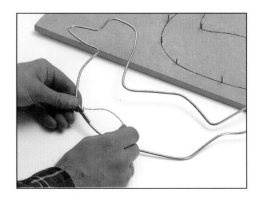

## STEP 1

To make a simple two-dimensional shape, draw the image on a board, then hammer small nails into place around the shape. You will need more nails to create detailed areas.

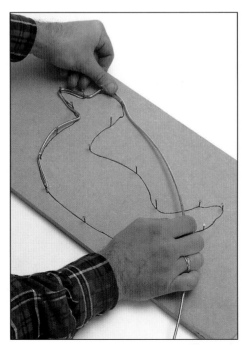

## STEP 4

Remove the wire frame from the nails, and flatten it out, if necessary. Secure the shape with fine wire.

## STEP 2

Using a straight piece of wire, start in the middle of the shape and bend it around the nails. It will help if you keep the wire flat with your other hand.

# THREE-DIMENSIONAL DOG FRAME

*The dog is one of the most popular frame designs for topiary. It may seem elaborate,*
*but is actually quite easy to make once you have learned how to join*
*the pieces of the frame together.*

## STEP 1

Plan out your design on paper to avoid making mistakes later. Transfer the designs onto your board and hammer in small nails in the same way as with two-dimensional designs.

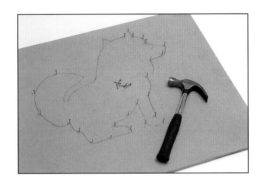

## STEP 2

Take a straight piece of heavy-duty wire and bend it around the nails to form the different shapes.

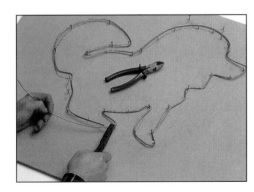

## STEP 3

Repeat the process with all your shapes. You can use the same board each time, as long as you don't want to repeat the design. Secure all the shapes with fine wire.

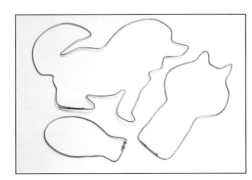

## STEP 4

To make the dog frame, take the back leg shape and wire it securely onto the body shape. Cover the binding wire with strong tape for extra rigidity and safety. Now take the front leg shape and repeat the process to complete the dog frame.

## STEP 5

The completed frame can be left as it is and plants can be trained over it, or it can be used as a base for a moss sculpture.

# CHICKEN WIRE TECHNIQUES

*Chicken wire makes an ideal base for your sculptures. It is fairly easy to cut and to bend, and with practice you will learn how to mold it with your hands to conform to the shape of your frame.*

### YOU WILL NEED
- Chicken wire
- Wire cutters or strong scissors
- Pliers
- Florist binding wire

### JOINING

To join two pieces of wire together, take a cut end from one piece and bend it several times around the other piece. The wire should be soft enough to bend by hand, but you can use a pair of pliers to secure it firmly.

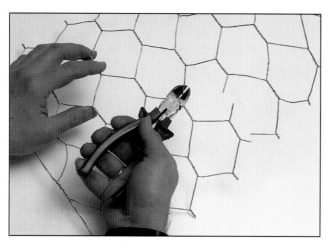

### CUTTING

If you have them, use wire cutters; otherwise use a very strong pair of scissors, but remember that cutting wire blunts scissors. Be careful once you have cut the chicken wire, since it will leave sharp ends exposed.

# COVERING A RIGID WIRE FRAME

*When you have made your frame you can cover it with chicken wire*
*and fill it with sphagnum moss to produce a solid base, which can either be left*
*as it is, or you can train plants over it.*

### STEP 1

To complete the three-dimensional dog sculpture, take some chicken wire and mold it around the rigid frame. Don't worry if the wire "doubles up" since this will help form the shape.

### STEP 2

Secure the chicken wire onto the frame with florist binding wire.

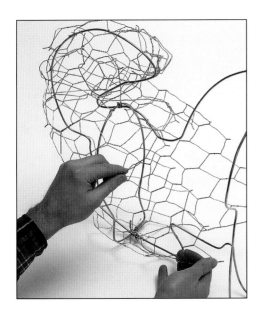

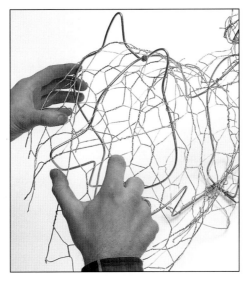

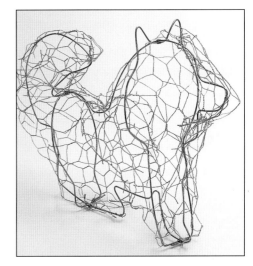

### STEP 3

Cut and join another length of of chicken wire, being careful to bend in all the loose sharp ends for safety.

### STEP 4

Continue to add chicken wire pieces until the frame is covered. Remember, if you are going to fill the frame with moss, you will need to leave some openings in the wire. These will be joined together once the shape has been filled.

# Plant Basics

Fresh and preserved plant material varies greatly. We have used the ideal material for each project and, where possible, have given a suitable alternative. This section provides general information and advice on the aftercare of plants and preserved materials.

## Fresh Plants

When choosing plants for topiary and green sculpture bear these points in mind:

**Size & Texture**   The size and texture of the plant should match the scale of the topiary. For small sculptures, use small-leaved plants that don't have heavy stems. Floor-standing sculptures need a plant with a strong central stem, especially if they don't have a supporting frame.

**Color**   Flowering plants provide welcome color, but don't ignore the wonderful variety of textured foliage plants, which can also produce very colorful results. If you are using flowering varieties, take note of the length and time of flowering, since you may find that some plants are suitable only at certain times of the year.

**Growth Rate**   There are quick ways for producing topiary, as we show in this book, but most topiary plants are slow to mature, so don't be in too much of a hurry to see the final results of your efforts.

**Growth Habits**   Plants with particular growth habits are needed for different types of sculpture. You need those that spread and cover easily for moss-filled shapes. For clipped topiary, plants that branch out when clipped or pinched are required. Vines or climbers that send out many tendrils are the most suitable for covering framework.

**Compatibility**   If you are making a group display, you must have plants that will flourish in similar conditions and require the same watering routine. If you want to create a particular effect, make sure you choose plants that best represent the texture.

## Drying & Preserving Plants

You can buy dried and preserved materials in an array of colors and forms, but it is quite easy to make your own by air-drying fresh plants in a cool, dry atmosphere, or by pressing plants and flowers between thick paper with heavy weights on top.

To preserve flowers, lay them in a container and cover them with fine sand, which will slowly absorb the moisture; or stand them in a mixture of glycerin and water. This is taken up by the stems and preserves the plants, while retaining their soft texture.

# TRAINING, PRUNING & CLIPPING

*Pruning and training details are given with each project, but there are basic methods for shaping and caring for topiary that will encourage growth.*

## WINDING

This is used mainly for ivies and vine-like plants that need little specialized care. Some are so vigorous that they will wind around the frame on their own. With others, you need gently to persuade the new growth to follow the frame shape.

## PINCHING OUT

This helps to maintain the plant's shape. Removing the shoot tips with the thumb and forefinger encourages the plant to make side growth and thicken up. It is specially effective on topiaries where cutting with tools would leave ugly marks.

## SECURING

Chiefly used for stronger stemmed plants, securing supports the stems and also ensures that the plants grow in the desired direction. You can use string, florist wire (plastic-coated, if possible) or garden ties to secure your plants. Do not bind them onto the frame too tightly, since this can damage their stems and restrict their growth.

## SHAPING

The process of shaping entails using a frame as a cutting guide to help you form a particular shape. The wire frame is placed over the plant, and removed when you have achieved the desired shape. This is a particularly useful technique for beginners.

## PRUNING

Use strong scissors or pruning shears. Regular clipping will encourage a plant to thicken out and form the desired shape. It also keeps an established plant shapely and healthy, preventing bare patches.

# REPOTTING A PLANT

*Plants should usually be moved into a pot only one size larger than the one they are in so that new roots will quickly penetrate the fresh potting soil. Make sure that the pot is well-drained and that you are using the right type of potting soil.*

### STEP 1

First, you must make sure that the drainage is good enough to prevent waterlogging, which can damage the plant's roots and may eventually kill it. If your container does not have drainage holes, you will need to make some. Then put some drainage material—either gravel or pottery shards—in the base of the pot or container.

### STEP 2

Add a suitable potting soil half way up the container. Different plants have different requirements, so check the growing instructions on each plant and select the right type of potting soil for it. Potting soils are either soil-based and contain loam, or soilless, usually containing a mixture of peat and sand, although today, many are made from peat substitutes. Specialized potting soils, such as orchid fiber and potting soil for hanging baskets, also exist.

### STEP 3

Stand the plant in the new pot to measure how high the potting soil must come.

**STEP 6**

Place the plant in the new container and add fresh potting soil around the rootball until it is about level with the bottom of the rim of the pot.

**STEP 4**

Place your hand on the potting soil surface, with the main stem, or stems, of the plant between your fingers. Turn the pot upside down and carefully remove it.

**STEP 5**

If the plant is rootbound, you may need to loosen the roots before replanting. This should be done very gently, loosening only those that come free easily.

**STEP 7**

Finally, press the potting soil down with your fingers. This will make sure the plant is firm and steady until a new root system is established. Then, water the pot well, and place it on a waterproof surface, or on a saucer with drainage.

# DRIED CARE & PRESERVATION
# TIPS & TECHNIQUES

*When using dried and preserved plant materials, there are some basic methods*
*you can apply to preparing, handling, securing, and aftercare.*

### WIRING
In most of the projects, the materials are bound together with wire, either singly or in small clusters to form much larger groups. This entails binding a sturdy length of wire around the stems and leaving some wire protruding to be inserted into the florist foam.

### YOU WILL NEED
• Strong scissors
• Wire cutters
• Long-bladed craft knife
• Selection of florist wire

### GLUING
Glue is useful to stick dried flowers into place without wiring them—dried flowers are fragile and you should handle them as little as possible. Even better than craft glue is a glue gun, which uses heated glue that sets very quickly, forming an instant bond. The glue can be extremely hot, so be careful when using a glue gun.

## WIRE HAIRPINNING

This method is used to attach moss onto foam, but it can also be adapted to pin into moss-filled shapes. Take a medium gauge wire about 4 inches (10 cm) long and bend it in the middle to form the hairpin. Use this to grip the moss.

## CLEANING

Dust, moisture, and direct sunlight can all adversely affect dried plants. Keeping them clean without damaging them is a particular problem. Preserved materials are less delicate and more supple and easier to clean, but even they need to be handled carefully.
The best way to clean both dried and preserved plants is to use a preserving and cleaning spray. This can be applied when the project is first completed, then used regularly to keep them clean and to reduce shedding. Alternatively, use a hairdryer on the lowest setting to gently remove the dust from a plant.

# SAFETY INFORMATION

Although topiary may seem the ideal relaxation hobby, you must be aware that the tools and materials used in these projects are potentially dangerous. However, if you follow a few simple rules you should be quite safe.

When making frames, be careful using the tools, especially when cutting wire. It is worth wearing protective gloves and glasses in case the wire springs back. Be especially aware of any sharp protruding ends. These can either be bent in for safety or blunted with a file. Be aware also of any rusty wire, and if you do cut yourself, seek medical advice. When using the glue gun it is a good idea to have a small bowl of cool water nearby. If you do drip hot glue onto your hands, dipping them into the water will cool the glue quickly and lessen the chance of a nasty burn.

The labels on plants should tell you whether they are poisonous, and all the plants we have used in these projects are harmless. However, even something as common as Hedera (ivy) can be toxic, so handle all plants with care. Wash your hands afterwards, and if any sort of irritation occurs, do not touch the plant again until you have sought medical advice.

This is also the case with fertilizers, which can be highly concentrated. You should read the safety advice on the container and never put your fingers near your mouth when handling fertilizers. Store them safely, preferably in the original container, to prevent mistakes.

Several of the plants used in these projects are large and heavy and they need to be handled correctly to avoid injury. Always ask for help if the item is too large for you to manage yourself. Take care not to strain your back by lifting badly—bend your knees to get down to the correct level. Remember that once the plant is placed in a container, it will be even heavier, so put it where it won't have to be moved often. Even lighter sculptures should be placed somewhere that will take their weight safely and which you can reach easily to maintain. Do not stand items on surfaces that will mark easily or that water may damage. Keep them well away from electrical equipment.

Although the projects in this book can be a lot of fun for children to try, it is not advisable for them to tackle the work unsupervised, and all the ingredients should be stored out of their reach so as to prevent any accidents from occurring.

# CUBES & SQUARES

Here we discover how creative and dramatic square and cube topiary shapes can be. These designs have a strong architectural flavor that creates a bold, geometric statement. Traditionally, very large squares, topiaries, and hedges have been cut from evergreens such as Taxus *(yew)* and Ilex *(holly)*, but in this chapter we show you how to scale down these ideas in order to make them more suitable for interiors, without losing any of their sharp-edged, dramatic appeal.

The pictures *(left)* illustrate some of the projects covered in this chapter and show details of a fragrant candleholder covered with aromatic dried spices such as cinnamon, aniseed, and cloves; an attractive display of Helxine soleirolii *(mind-your-own-business)* trailing naturally over similar, square-shaped containers; regimented, dried heads of golden wheat in a simple and striking display; and a square-clipped, floor-standing, living Buxus microphylla *(boxwood)* topiary.

# ROSEMARY CUBE

*This is a beautiful fresh arrangement for adorning a windowsill or kitchen counter. Clipped simply to shape and arranged in different-sized pots, these cubes will transform a dull-looking corner.*

## STEP 1

Plant as shown in Plant Basics (*see* pp.22-23). Clip back the side shoots with scissors to start the shape. Taking off just a little at a time, trim the sides of the plant evenly, until you have a shape that follows the lines of the pot.

## STEP 2

Clip the top in a similar way to finish the cube. Water well and place in a sunny spot, such as a kitchen windowsill.

## INGREDIENTS

- Square terracotta pot
- Soil-based potting soil
- Pottery shards or other drainage material
- Scissors
- Secateurs

## THE PLANT

- *Rosmarinus officinalis* (rosemary)

The plant should be bushy and low-growing with plenty of straight stems.

## ALTERNATIVE

- *Buxus microphylla* (boxwood)

## AFTERCARE

Water well in summer and sparingly in winter. Turn the plant occasionally to encourage even growth. Trim, or pinch, new shoots on the top and sides regularly to keep the shape. This will also stimulate new growth, and prevent the plant from becoming woody.

# TRAILING HELXINE

*This is an attractive plant that will trail naturally over a square/cubed container to produce a stylish column. Several plants arranged together on a dining table would look stunning in a modern setting.*

## STEP 1

Place drainage gravel in the bottom of the container and fill halfway with suitable potting soil. Remove the plant from its original pot by placing your hand over the top and inverting it. Lift the pot from the root ball, being careful not to damage any fine roots. Gently tease out the roots to encourage them to take in the new soil.

## INGREDIENTS
- 12 inch (30 cm) tall, stylish square/cubed container
- Multi-purpose potting soil
- Drainage gravel

## THE PLANT
- *Helxine soleirolii* syn. *Soleirolia soleirolii* (baby's tears, mind-your-own-business)

## ALTERNATIVE
- *Nertera granadensis* (bead plant)

## AFTERCARE
This plant needs to be kept moist at all times, so water it well and mist the leaves frequently to prevent the top from drying out. *Helxine* likes plenty of light but will tolerate some shade. No special training is required, since it will grow down the sides of the container naturally. Trim off any straggly trailing stems.

## STEP 2

Place the plant in the new pot. Lift up the sides of the plant to fill the container with more potting soil handling the trails gently to avoid damage. Press the potting soil down firmly with your fingers. Water the plant thoroughly.

# BOXWOOD BOXES

*Clipped into a neat geometric shape, this glossy, tight-leaved plant will produce a living sculpture suitable for a light, airy situation, such as a sunroom or conservatory.*

### STEP 1

Choose a mature five- to six-year-old plant. It should have a strong central stem and be quite bushy, to give it a head start. Plant it in a container that has plenty of room for several years' growth, then cut a shape with scissors or pruning shears, but be careful not to cut off too much at one time.

### STEP 2

Continue to refine the shape. It is better to cut back just a little at a time rather than cutting back too much. Keeping the pruning shears flat to the topiary will help to create a sharp form; this may take some practice. Cover the soil with decorative stones, which also help to retain the moisture.

### INGREDIENTS

- Suitable large container
- Soil-based potting soil
- Drainage material
- Pruning shears and/or strong scissors
- Decorative stones

### THE PLANT

- *Buxus microphylla* (boxwood)

### ALTERNATIVE

- *Viburnum tinus* (laurustinus)

### AFTERCARE

When trimming the plant, don't cut out the leading shoots, but trim the tips to encourage the plant to thicken out. Although boxwood will grow in a light, cool interior, it benefits from an occasional "vacation" outdoors.

# COLORED CUBES

*Beautifully colored, preserved flat leaves are used to create stacked cubes. This multi-textured sculptural display makes a stylish addition to a sideboard or table.*

### STEP 1

Before you start this project, flatten the leaves under paper and weights. Cut the florist foam into large cubes. Cover these bases with cardboard and felt and secure the cubes together with short wires and glue.

### STEP 2

Start covering a cube with one type of leaf. Use glue and florist wire hairpins (*see* p.25) or needlework pins. Make sure each new leaf overlaps the last, so the pins don't show.

### STEP 3

Cover the top and sides of the cubes and trim the edges with sharp scissors. Add interest to your design by using leaves with different textures for each cube.

### INGREDIENTS

- Florist foam for dried flowers
- Sharp knife
- Glue gun or quick-drying glue
- Scissors
- Medium gauge florist wire
- Hairpins/needlework pins
- Felt material
- Stiff cardboard

### THE PLANTS

Any flat, preserved leaves such as those of:
- Magnolia
- Salal
- Galax
- Oak
- Beech

### AFTERCARE

Preserved leaves keep their color and suppleness much longer than traditional dried leaves and can be wiped clean with a cloth without being damaged. Place this display on a mat because, in warm conditions, the leaves may leak preservatives, which can stain.

# VELVET OBELISK

*The velvet obelisk is a column covered with richly colored preserved moss, set on a velvet base and tied with gold cord to make an opulent and luxurious shelf decoration.*

### STEP 1

Cut the dried foam into an obelisk shape with a sharp knife. Glue it into a base container, such as a plant pot.

### STEP 2

Pin the moss to the foam with wire hairpins (*see* p.25). Keeping the moss closely packed, work from the top downward.

### STEP 3

Follow the line of the foam to produce a crisp shape, keeping the moss as even as possible. When the foam is completely covered, glue on the velvet to finish off the base. Finally, for a touch of luxury, add the gold cord around the base.

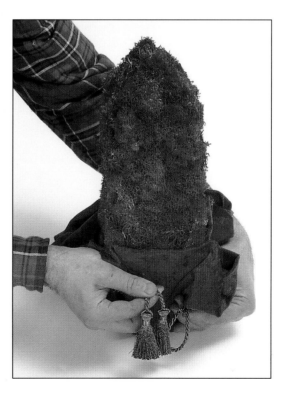

### INGREDIENTS

- Florist foam for dried flowers
- Small square container for base
- Velvet material, gold cord with tassel
- Sharp knife
- Scissors
- Glue gun with quick-drying glue
- Light and medium gauge florist wire

### THE PLANT

- Preserved 'reindeer' moss

### ALTERNATIVE

- Spanish moss

### AFTERCARE

Spray the plant with preservative spray or cleaner for dried flowers. If any dust settles, either spray again or gently blow the arrangement with a hairdryer. Keep the display out of direct sunlight to prevent it from fading.

# SPICE BOX

*Covering a cube with dried spices, such as cinnamon, aniseed, and cloves, makes a richly-colored decorative display that will fill a room with subtle aromatic scents.*

### STEP 1

Cut the florist foam into a cube shape. Attach the wooden base with glue. Spray both cube and base with several thin coats of paint, and when it is dry, press the candleholder into the foam.

### STEP 2

Start gluing or pressing the dried spices onto the foam base. Arrange them as close together as possible, but don't worry if some press into the foam or there are small spaces, as the gold paint will show through. Make blocks of each of the different materials to create a geometric pattern.

### STEP 3

Cover the cube, leaving a small area for the candle to be inserted into the holder. This is a candleholder, but do not let the candle burn down into the arrangement.

## INGREDIENTS
• Florist foam for dried flowers
• Sharp knife
• Glue gun or quick-drying glue
• Small wooden base
• Gold spray paint
• Candleholder
• Pillar candle

## THE PLANTS
Any of the following:
• Cloves
• Bay leaves
• Cinnamon sticks
• Aniseed pods

## ALTERNATIVES
Dried apple or orange slices

## AFTERCARE
Never leave the candles burning unattended. Once the natural scents of the spices have faded, potpourri oils can be added to give the display a new lease of life.

# WHEAT SCULPTURE

*Golden wheat trimmed and blocked in a copper trough makes an attractive display, suitable for areas too dried or dark for living plants.*

### STEP 1

Prepare the container by cutting the florist foam to shape and gluing it in. If you are using a basket, secure the foam with florist wires bent over and pushed through the sides. The florist foam should sit one inch (2.5 cm) below the rim of the container.

### STEP 2

Remove any leaves from the stalks of wheat so that only a clean stem and the head remain. Starting at one end of the florist foam, push the wheat vertically into the foam so that all the heads are at the same level and the stems are parallel.

### STEP 3

Continue until the foam is covered, placing the stems of wheat in strict rows to produce a very even design. Add moss around the edge of the wheat and finish it off with a braided paper ribbon tie.

## INGREDIENTS
- Florist foam for dried flowers
- Sharp knife
- Glue gun or quick-drying glue
- Rectangular copper container (could be plastic, ceramic, or basketware)
- Moss
- Paper ribbon
- Scissors

## THE PLANT
- Golden wheat

## ALTERNATIVES
- Poppy heads
- Barley

## AFTERCARE

If this sculpture is kept in a place where humidity is high, the dried heads will deteriorate quickly, so keep it away from steam and heat. Remove any dust by blowing it carefully with a hairdryer, or use a specialist cleaning spray.

# SPIRALS & CONES

The projects covered in this chapter represent not only the classical forms used in formal topiary structures, but demonstrate how, with the use of new and inspiring materials, a contemporary look can also easily be achieved. We look at designs on different scales, from detailed table-top displays to impressive floor-standing sculptures. The pictures (left) are details of some of the projects covered in this chapter such as sweet-smelling preserved lavender set in a traditional, antique effect, urn-shaped container; exotic glory lily trained around a spiral frame; delicate, fragrant jasmine growing around a triangular frame; and imitation boxwood spiraling around a central pole to create a modern sculpture.

# BOXWOOD CONE

*There are various ways to create a boxwood cone. If you have a good eye, you can clip the shape freehand. Otherwise, you can make your own frame, or buy a prefabricated one.*

## INGREDIENTS
- Terracotta pot (or similar weighted container)
- Suitable soil
- Drainage material
- Pruning shears
- Scissors
- Bun moss
- Ornamental stones

## THE PLANT
- *Buxus microphylla* (boxwood—choose a tree 3-4 years old)

## ALTERNATIVES
- Conifers
- *Laurus nobilis* (sweet bay)

## AFTERCARE
This plant will provide temporary winter color indoors, but is unsuitable as a permanent feature. It will do better in a light sun porch or sunroom—but be careful that the leaves do not become scorched from too much heat in summer. It will need clipping or pinching two or three times a year.

### STEP 1
Transfer the mature tree into a new, more permanent container, being careful not to damage the rootball. Water it well after repotting. When the plant has started to grow again, begin pruning and clipping. Clip back the lower growth to reveal the central main stem, and trim any branches that are below the base of the cone shape.

## STEP 2

Clip any excess growth to make a clean shape. If you need a guide, place a wire frame over the top of the tree and remove it when you have obtained an accurate shape. Pinching stem tips may be better in some places, since clipping can leave marks on the leaves. Cover the soil with bun moss and ornamental stones to give the topiary a finished look and to help keep the soil moist.

# Triangular Jasmine Tree

*Delicate, sweet-smelling jasmine, planted in an attractive container and encouraged to trail over a triangular frame, will brighten up any room, especially in winter.*

### Step 1

Make a two-dimensional frame shape (*see* Making Frames, p.16). Place drainage material in the bottom of the container and fill it halfway with potting soil. Remove the jasmine from its old pot and plant it in the new container, being careful not to damage the root ball, and firm the potting soil down with your fingers. Place the wire frame over the center of the plant, and push the legs firmly into the potting soil.

### Step 2

Wind the jasmine trails up and around the frame, attaching them as you go with wire or ties. Don't make these too tight or you will damage the stems. Water well, and place the plant in a setting with good light.

### Ingredients

- Suitable container
- Potting soil
- Drainage material
- Two-dimensional wire frame
- Florist wire or garden ties
- Scissors

### The plant

- *Jasminum polyanthum* (pink jasmine)

### Alternatives

- *Stephanotis floribunda* (stephanotis)
- *Ceropegia woodii* (rosary vine)

### Aftercare

Remove old flower heads. As new growth appears, tie back the shoots with wire. Keep the plant in a cool place, and if possible stand it outside in summer. Do not let the compost dry out, and spray the leaves with water occasionally.

# Conifer Twist

*An impressive display can be made by clipping a conifer to form a spiral. This dramatic topiary would be ideal to stand on the floor in a bright hallway or a sunroom.*

### Step 1

Choose a young, bushy plant, as this will regrow better. It should also be tall and narrow for this type of topiary. Using string or a piece of fine rope, start at the top and spiral it down around the tree. It may take several attempts to get this right, but since the string will act as a cutting guide, it is important to get the spacing correct.

### Step 2

Cut back all the branches that lie in the path of the string to the central stem. This forms the basis of the spiral.

## STEP 3

Cut back the tips of any remaining branches to create a smooth outline. This will also encourage growth and thicken up the foliage so that it forms the correct shape. Do not leave the plant in strong sunlight, especially when it has been newly trimmed.

## INGREDIENTS
- Large stone or terracotta pot
- Suitable potting soil
- Dainage material
- Scissors
- Pruning shears
- String or fine rope

## THE PLANT
Most types of conifer, for example,
- *Thuja occidentalis* 'Emerald' (white cedar)

## ALTERNATIVE
- *Ligustrum ovalifolium* 'Aureum' (golden privet)

## AFTERCARE
This plant likes plenty of light and should be brought inside for only 3-4 weeks at a time. Misting and regular watering will help to prevent the plant from drying out. To retain the shape, repeat the clipping process as side shoots develop during the growing season.

# SPIRALING GLORIOSA

*This exotic plant of the lily family is trained around a spiral frame to create a glamorous alternative to the usual trailing houseplants.*

## STEP 1

This spiral can be grown from a tuber, but the lily will need support as it grows, since the stems are quite fine. An established plant will make an outstanding instant display. Start by untangling the plant from the original supports and spreading out the trailing stems. Push the new frame firmly into the potting soil. Twine the stems around the frame, attaching them with wire or ties.

## STEP 2

Continue tying in the trails until the frame is covered. Do not attach them too tightly or you will damage the stems; the ties serve only to train the plant in the right direction, and this should be quite a free-flowing design. Place in a decorative outer pot and cover the soil with the pebbles or gravel. Attach the new growth as it develops, making the spiral look as wild as you wish.

### INGREDIENTS
- Decorative pot (or outer pot)
- Prefabricated spiral frame
- Lightweight florist wire or garden ties
- Decorative pebbles or gravel
- Scissors

### THE PLANT
- *Gloriosa rothschildiana* (glory lily)

### ALTERNATIVE
- *Plumbago auriculata* (Cape leadwort)

### AFTERCARE
Tie in the trails as they develop—the stem ends tend to attach themselves very firmly and can be difficult to untangle. After the flowering season, the foliage will die back, and the tuber may be stored for repotting in the spring.

# LAVENDER URN

*A compact pyramid topiary of preserved lavender, arranged in an antique-effect cast-iron urn, will transform an ordinary hallway into an elegant, sweetly perfumed entrance.*

### STEP 1

Use a prefabricated foam cone, or cut a block into shape with a sharp knife. Secure the block firmly in the container, using a hot glue gun or quick-drying glue. Wire the lavender into short bunches with florist wire (*see* p.24). This helps to support the lavender and prevents the stems from snapping as it is pushed into the foam.

### STEP 2

Starting at the top of the cone and working your way down the sides, push in small bunches of lavender. These will serve as a guide for the overall final shape.

### STEP 3

Continue to cover the foam, keeping the bunches close together to form a mass of flower heads. Keep the outline as even as possible, and trim off any stray pieces when you have finished.

### INGREDIENTS

- Metal urn or other similar container
- Florist foam for dried flowers (cone or block shape)
- Sharp knife
- Medium gauge florist wire
- Glue gun or quick-drying glue
- Scissors

### THE PLANT

- Lavender bunches (dried or preserved)

### ALTERNATIVE

- Dyed wheat

### AFTERCARE

Use a preserving spray if possible, and gently blow away any dust with a hairdryer. Lavender fragrance or essential oil can be added to the flower heads when the original scent has faded.

# SUNDRIED FRUIT SCULPTURE

*A mound of pinecones, artificial fruits, and preserved leaves in a fine glass vase makes a beautiful alternative Christmas tree. Place a pair on either side of a mantelpiece for greater impact.*

### STEP 1
Fill the base of the container with a selection of the fruits, cones, and leaves. Cut the foam into a small pyramid to fit the neck of your container; if the base shows, cover it with leaves. Glue the foam in place.

### STEP 2
Wire the cones and fruits in small groups (*see* p.24) and push them into the foam. Secure heavy items with glue.

### STEP 3
Cover the cone with a selection of your materials. Small clusters look much better than single items. Fill any small gaps between them with leaves.

## INGREDIENTS
- Glass container
- Florist foam for dried flowers
- Medium gauge florist wire
- Glue gun or quick-drying glue
- Scissors

## THE PLANTS
A selection of cones, preserved leaves, artificial fruits, and berries—perhaps small amounts left over from other projects.

## ALTERNATIVES
- Mixed nuts

## AFTERCARE
Some artificial items and preserved leaves can be damaged by direct sunlight or heat, so be careful where you place this arrangement.

# IMITATION BOXWOOD SPIRAL

*Boxwood foliage is ideal for creating this modern sculpture for a dark corner in which houseplants would not survive. The cut foliage is clipped in the traditional way and will dry naturally.*

## INGREDIENTS

- Tall outer galvanized bucket or metal vase
- Plastic container (to fit inside outer container)
- Wooden pole 1-1½ inches (2.5-3.8 cm) in diameter
- Quick-drying plaster
- Chicken wire
- Heavy duty florist wire
- Staple gun
- String
- Scissors

## THE PLANT

- *Buxus microphylla* (boxwood)

## ALTERNATIVES

- Conifers

## AFTERCARE

Once the foliage has dried out, it will fade, but you can spray it with natural green spray paint to improve the color if you wish.

### STEP 1

Cut the pole to the height you want the final sculpture. Set it in plaster in a plastic pot to avoid damaging the outer pot. You may need to support the pole while the plaster is drying to make sure that it stays vertical. Place the plastic pot in the outer container and attach chicken wire to the pole with a staple gun, making a cone shape.

### STEP 2

Make another cone of chicken wire and lay it on top of the first. These form the base into which the foliage will be inserted.

### STEP 3

Cut the foliage into short-stemmed pieces and stuff small bunches of it into the chicken wire.

### STEP 4

Completely cover the chicken wire base with an even layer of the foliage to form a rough cone shape. The foliage should be densely packed so that it won't fall out.

### STEP 5

Spiral a piece of string around the cone to act as a cutting guide. Then, following the string, clip back the foliage to make a spiral groove.

### STEP 6

Do not cut too much at a time, and keep turning the sculpture to get an even shape. Remove the string and smooth out the edges and curves to produce a graduated spiral.

# SPHERES & CIRCLES

This chapter looks at ways of creating designs using spherical and circular shapes. These are particularly good for the home, since their soft, harrmonious outlines are pleasing and restful to the eye. Single and multi-ball standard topiaries have been popular for centuries in garden design, and here we show you how to transfer these ideas into successful interior decorations. Circle and ball shapes are most suitable for rapidly growing plants because it is easier to keep the display following the shape of the topiary than it is with some of the more complicated forms. The pictures (left) illustrate details of the topiaries in this chapter including different types of foliage in fall colors used to produce a rich, earthy display; different-sized balls of moss used to make a sculpture on a pole; a living plant garland of stephanotis and grape ivy for Christmas; and a topiary ball of sweet bay, with oranges and cinnamon sticks added, for a special occasion.

# IVY BALL

*This is a quick way of covering a "lollipop" frame with trailing plants to make a decoration suitable for a tabletop or to stand on the floor.*

## INGREDIENTS

- Terracotta pot or similar medium-sized container
- Wire ball (lollipop) frame
- Soil-based potting soil
- Florist wire or garden ties
- Bun moss and stones

## THE PLANTS

- *Hedera* spp. (ivy), 2 or 3 trailing plants, one with variegated leaves.

## ALTERNATIVE

- *Rhoicissus rhomboidea* (grape ivy)

## AFTERCARE

These are some of the easiest plants to care for and they will tolerate most conditions. Don't forget to water all the plants and mist them regularly to stop the leaves from browning. This display needs regular training to keep its shape and to encourage it to cover the frame completely.

## STEP 1

Place the ball frame into the pot, and fill halfway with potting soil. Plant one of the ivies, add potting soil until it is level with the bottom of the pot rim. Spread out the trails of the ivy.

## STEP 2

Place the other plants inside the ball frame, and secure the plants to the top of the frame with wire.

### STEP 3

Train the lower plant up the stem of the ball and secure it where necessary.

### STEP 4

Pull the stems of the upper plants through the frame to cover the ball, using wire to keep them in place. Mix the two types of ivy for dramatic effect. Water the plants well, and cover the soil with moss and stones.

# CHRISTMAS RING

*Use this decorative ring to dress up your existing topiaries, or make it for the festive season. It could also be adapted to form a high-table centerpiece for a wedding or other special event.*

### STEP 1

Plant both plants in a suitable container with drainage material and potting soil. Push the ring frame into the potting soil in the center of the pot, between the plants, being careful not to damage them. Wind the ivy around the frame, securing it with wire, quite loosely, but tightly enough to support the plant and stop it from springing back.

### STEP 2

Thread the stephanotis through the ivy so that the two plants are evenly distributed around the ring.

### STEP 3

Decorate the ring, using wired cones, gilded berries, and a decorative bow, to create a growing seasonal garland.

### INGREDIENTS

- Decorative container
- Potting soil
- Drainage material
- Two-dimensional, strong wire frame
- Florist wire or ties
- Christmas decorations or decorative berries and cones

### THE PLANTS

- *Stephanotis floribunda* (stephanotis)
- *Rhoicissus rhomboidea* (grape ivy)

### ALTERNATIVE

- *Passiflora caerulea* (passion flower)

### AFTERCARE

If you keep this beautiful display moist and in a warm (not hot) room, it will flower for several weeks. It will stay green long after flowering if you remove any dead flowers. The plants need regular training.

# MOSS BALL & CLIMBER

*This lush arrangement is made by training a climbing plant over a moss ball base. The addition of some dogwood twigs gives a modern, natural texture to the sculpture.*

## INGREDIENTS
- Wire frame
- Chicken wire
- Green spray paint
- Sphagnum moss
- Strong florist reel wire
- Medium gauge florist wire or garden ties
- Suitable container
- Soil-based potting soil
- Drainage materials

## THE PLANTS
- *Hedera* spp. (ivy)
- Dogwood twigs softened in water

## ALTERNATIVE
- *Thunbergia alata* (black-eyed Susan)

## AFTERCARE
Keep the moss moist at all times. This climber grows very quickly and needs regular training and trimming, otherwise it will grow out of shape.

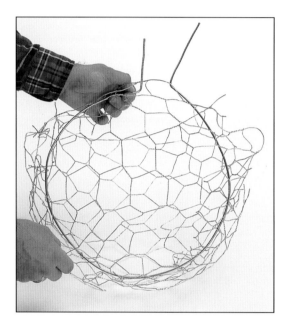

## STEP 1
Cover a simple circle frame with chicken wire to form a ball, leaving an opening, and leave the wire ends free. Spray paint the frame to give it a better apppearance.

## STEP 2
Stuff the ball with moist moss, packing it down hard to give it a rigid base.

### STEP 3

Plant the ivy in the
new container, leaving
a space in the center
for the ball.

### STEP 4

Push the moss ball
firmly into the potting
soil. Start trailing the
stems over the ball
and securing them
with wire hairpins
(*see* p.25).

## STEP 5

Cover the ball with the remaining ivy stems as evenly as possible.

## STEP 6

Add some softened dogwood twigs around the ball to produce a natural-looking sculpture. Secure the twigs to the frame with wire to prevent them from springing out.

# CELEBRATION BAY TREE

*Decorating a standard ball bay tree with fruit and scented cinnamon sticks quickly turns a plain plant into a colorful and festive topiary for any occasion.*

### STEP 1

Repot the tree, or simply place it in a decorative outer pot—line it inside with plastic to stop water from seeping through. Otherwise, cover the container with suitable material, securing it with a raffia tie.

### STEP 2

Bind the fruit, cinnamon sticks, and any other decorative items with raffia or colorful string. (If you bind the fruit carefully, you can use it later.) Tie these pieces to the stronger branches of the tree, making sure not to overload the branches.

## STEP 3

Decorate the pot in a similar way to finish off your design.

### INGREDIENTS

- Decorative pot
- Material for covering the pot
- Oranges or lemons
- Cinnamon sticks and other decorative items
- Raffia or colorful string

### THE PLANT

- *Laurus nobilis* (sweet bay), large enough to support the weight of the fruit.

### ALTERNATIVE

- *Ficus benjamina* (weeping fig)

### AFTERCARE

After the big occasion, remove the decorations and keep the tree in cool conditions indoors or in a sunny place outdoors. It could be decorated for many occasions. Threaded with colored lights, it would make an attractive alternative to conifers for Christmas.

# MOSS BALL POLE

*Using bun moss to cover three different-sized moss ball frames makes a striking tree sculpture to stand in a dark corner unsuitable for fresh plants.*

### STEP 1

Cut a pole to the height you want the finished sculpture and set it in plaster in the pot. When the plaster is dry, attach chicken wire to the pole with a staple gun or nails. Create a ball of chicken wire around the base of the pole.

### STEP 2

Stuff the chicken wire with sphagnum moss to create a hard ball. Repeat the process to make two more balls, each of which should be smaller than the last.

## STEP 3

Attach small pieces of the bun moss firmly to the sphagnum moss balls with wire hairpins (*see* p.25). Cover the balls completely to create a soft carpet of moss.

### INGREDIENTS
- Terracotta pot or similar weighted pot
- Wooden pole 1-1½ inches (2.5-3.8 cm) in diameter
- Quick-drying plaster
- Chicken wire
- Staple gun
- Sphagnum moss
- Medium gauge florist wire
- Scissors

### THE PLANT
- *Leucobryum glaucum* (bun moss)

### ALTERNATIVE
- Preserved 'reindeer' moss

### AFTERCARE
If you keep this tree moist, it should keep its fresh green color. Otherwise, it dries naturally to pale green, but will regain its fresh color if you rewet it.

# PURE & SIMPLE

*The clean lines of this elegant sculpture make it perfect for a bathroom. A globe of preserved white roses is set on a wooden pole and placed in a glass tank filled with shells, sand, or pebbles.*

### STEP 1

Set the stem in plaster in the small container and allow it to dry. Place the stem inside the larger glass container and add shells, sand, or pebbles to hide the inner pot.

### STEP 2

Fix the foam ball to the top of the pole with glue. Start to add the roses, gluing them to the foam for extra security.

### STEP 3

Continue to add roses to the foam ball, making sure they are packed tightly together.

### INGREDIENTS

- Large glass container
- Small container
- Wooden pole 1-1½ inches (2.5-3.8 cm) in diameter, or a twisted branch
- Quick-drying plaster
- Quick-drying glue
- Florist foam ball for dried flowers
- Shells, sand, or pebbles

### THE PLANT

- Preserved roses (These do not lose their color and stay soft to the touch)

### ALTERNATIVE

- Dried rose heads

### AFTERCARE

Dried roses will deteriorate rapidly in a very humid place, such as a bathroom, so if you use them, keep the sculpture in a dry place.

# Autumn Fireball

*A large and impressive globe topiary of mixed preserved leaves in rich colors of bronze, gold, burgundy, and rust creates a wonderful reminder of autumn splendor. Scent completes the effect.*

### Step 1

Put a few stones in the bottom of the smaller pot, set the pole in plaster and leave it to dry. Push the foam ball onto the pole and glue it securely. Add fine twigs around the pole and fix them with wire, top and bottom. Weave a few of the twigs into the others to cover the pole completely.

### Step 2

Cut the preserved foliage into small sprigs, with three to five leaves on each. Push them into the foam, gluing them, if necessary. Keep turning the arrangement to achieve an even shape overall.

### Step 3

Completely cover the ball with leaves, grouping leaves of the same kind into small clusters to create a stronger design. Fill any small gaps with odd leaves. Cover the top of the pot with potpourri to give your fireball a beautiful aroma.

## Ingredients

- Decorative container
- Smaller container
- Wooden pole 1-1½ inches (2.5-3.8 cm) in diameter
- Quick-drying plaster
- Stones for weight
- Florist foam ball for dried flowers
- Glue gun or quick-drying glue
- Medium gauge florist wire
- Scissors
- Fine twigs
- Potpourri

## The plants

- Dried or preserved leaves of oak, beech, or eucalyptus

## Alternatives

- Ivy, horse chestnut, or *Gaultheria shallon* (salal, shallon)

## Aftercare

Preserved leaves neither dry out nor fade, but it is best to keep them out of direct sunlight. Use a specialized cleaner spray or blow off dust with a cool hairdryer.

# FREEFORM DISPLAYS

Let your imagination run riot and create the wild, fantastical, and amusing. By following the basic techniques described in this chapter, you will be able to make the sculptures shown here. You will also acquire the skills that you will need to design and create your own unique sculptures, which you can use to decorate your home or which can become a fabulous centerpiece on a table for a special occasion or celebration. The illustrations (left) show details of some of the projects covered in this chapter including two types of Ficus pumila (creeping fig) trained over an interesting and amusing moss frame; a stylish display of traditional dried flower balls arranged in an unconventional manner around twisted stems of willow; and a group display of flowering plants, including a standard tree of mixed florists' chrysanthemums and foliage dressed for a wedding, dramatic amaryllis, and an exotic white moth orchid.

# CREEPING FIG SCULPTURE

*The easiest way to cover a moss sculpture is with creeping figs, since they cling so well. This project shows how to combine two varieties of figs and could be adapted to create any shape.*

## INGREDIENTS
- Suitable container
- Potting soil
- Drainage material
- Strong wire frame
- Medium gauge florist wire
- Scissors
- Fishing line
- Chicken wire
- Green spray paint
- Sphagnum moss

## THE PLANTS
- *Ficus pumila* (creeping fig), one plain, one variegated

## ALTERNATIVES
- *Hedera* spp. (ivy), small-leaved varieties

## AFTERCARE
It is important that the moss and potting soil are kept moist at all times. Mist the plant regularly to prevent the leaves browning. Train and pin in stems frequently to keep the shape.

### STEP 1
Make the base frame with strong wire (*see* Making Frames pp. 14-19).

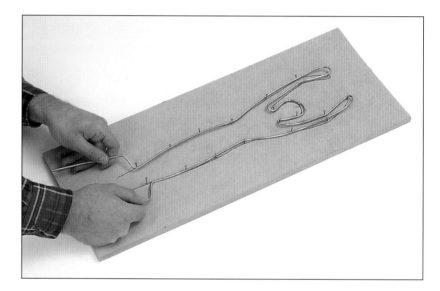

### STEP 2
Cover the frame with damp moss. You can bind this on with florist wire, but for a better finish use fishing line. The moss should be quite firm.

### STEP 3

Make a ball with the chicken wire and wire it to the moss figure. You can spray paint the ball to give it a better appearance. Fill the ball with damp moss. Now add a second pair of legs to the frame for extra stability.

### STEP 4

Fill the container with drainage material and potting soil. Make sure the potting soil is firm, and push the figure into it.

### STEP 5

Fill the center of the moss ball with potting soil and plant one of the creeping figs in it.

**STEP 6**

Train and secure the stems with hairpins made from florist wire (*see* p.25).

**STEP 7**

Plant the second creeping fig in the lower pot and train the stems over the damp moss. Follow the lines of the sculpture as closely as you can.

# IVY CANDELABRA

*This candelabra, wreathed in variegated trailing ivies and with the candles, makes it an unusual and memorable centerpiece for a dinner party table.*

### STEP 2

Put drainage material and potting soil into the pot, and plant sections of the ivies around the edge. Push the frame into the potting soil in the center of the pot, making sure it is secure, because it will be holding candles.

### INGREDIENTS

- Decorative pot
- Potting soil
- Drainage material
- Metal frame with candleholders and candles
- Medium gauge florist wire or ties

### THE PLANTS

- *Hedera* spp. (ivy), preferably two different varieties

### ALTERNATIVES

- Any trailing ivies and vines *Rhoicissus rhomboidea* (grape ivy)

### AFTERCARE

If you use this candelabra on a table, stand the pot on a mat. Although this design can be made for a special occasion, it will grow happily on this frame for years. Keep the soil moist and spray the leaves regularly. Once the plants are established, winding the new growth back into the main stems will keep them in place.

### STEP 1

If possible, divide larger plants into smaller sections by shaking excess soil from the rootball and gently pulling the roots apart. This will be easier if you water the plant an hour or so beforehand.

### STEP 3

Trail the plants up the frame, securing them with wire or ties as you go, but never tying too tightly. Intersperse the two types of ivy for the most attractive effect. Moss can be added to cover any potting soil that shows through.

# MIXED PLANT SCULPTURE

*This striking animal sculpture is made by using a wire and chicken wire frame. By filling it with moss you can plant your sculpture as you would a hanging basket.*

## INGREDIENTS
• Heavy wire frame
• Chicken wire
• Sphagnum moss
• Potting soil
• Fishing line
• Medium gauge florist wire
• Dish with pebbles or gravel

## THE PLANTS
• *Chlorophytum comosum* (spider plant)
• *Fittonia verschaffeltii* 'Nana' (silver net leaf)
• *Hypoestes phyllostachya* (polka dot plant)
• *Pilea cadierei* (aluminum plant)

## ALTERNATIVES
•*Hedera* spp. (ivy)
•*Nertera granadensis* (bead plant)

## AFTERCARE
If you put the sculpture on a dish filled with wet pebbles, it will not require such frequent watering, as water is absorbed by the moss. Otherwise keep the moss and potting soil damp and spray the plants regularly.

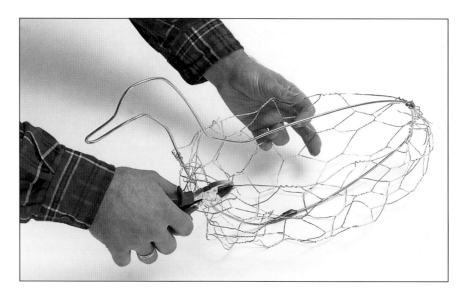

### STEP 1
You will need to make a strong metal base frame; the rest of the shape is made with chicken wire (*see* Making Frames pp. 14-19). Leave sections of the chicken wire frame open so that it can be filled with moss.

### STEP 2
Fill the larger areas of the frame with damp moss, and use fishing line to attach the other, smaller parts to the moss.

### STEP 3

Make a depression in the body and fill it with potting soil, packing it quite firmly in order to keep the shape of the sculpture.

### STEP 4

Set the plants in the potting soil so as to mimic the different textures and markings of a bird's feathers.

## STEP 5

Add plants at the sides of the body by inserting them through the moss. If you first make a hole in the moss with a pencil, the plants' roots will not be damaged. Seal with moss.

## STEP 6

Cover any visible potting soil with moss to help retain moisture. Stand the sculpture on a dish of pebbles to water it.

# CLIPPED BOXWOOD SCULPTURE

*Made from a chicken wire frame, stuffed with leaves and then clipped, this challenging display will be easy to achieve once you have mastered the techniques of topiary clipping.*

**STEP 1**

Attach the pole to the wooden base with screws or brackets. Cover the pole with a layer of chicken wire, securing it to the center pole and the base with a staple gun.

**STEP 2**

Cover the first layer of chicken wire with a second layer, again fixing it firmly to the pole and base. Shape both layers to your rough design.

**STEP 3**

Cut the boxwood foliage into short sections and, following the design shape, push small compact bunches of leaves into the chicken wire.

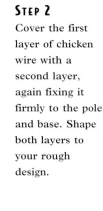

**STEP 4**

With scissors or pruning shears, gradually trim the sculpture until it matches the size and shape of your original design.

### INGREDIENTS

- Wooden pole 1-1½ inches (2.5-3.8 cm) in diameter
- Screws or brackets
- Wooden base
- Chicken wire
- Staple gun
- Pruning shears or scissors
- Green spray paint

### THE PLANT

- Fresh cut foliage of *Buxus microphylla* (boxwood)

### ALTERNATIVE

- Cut conifer foliage

### AFTERCARE

The foliage will gradually dry out but, if you wish, it can be sprayed with green paint once it fades. Do not keep the sculpture in a damp location, since mold can develop.

# MULTI-BALL TREE

*A quirky, yet stylish, display of dried flower balls arranged around stems of twisted willow, this makes a great focal point for a living or dining room.*

### INGREDIENTS
- Decorative pot and stones
- Quick-drying plaster
- Twisted stems of willow or hazel
- Florist foam balls for dried flowers (various sizes)
- Florist tape
- Medium gauge florist wire,
- Scissors
- Glue gun or quick-drying glue

### THE PLANT
- Mixed dried flower heads of *Helichrysum bracteatum* (everlasting, strawflower)

### ALTERNATIVES
- Dried flower heads of nigella or hydrangea

### AFTERCARE
Keep dried and preserved materials out of direct sun and away from heat. To save the flower balls for another occasion, secure plastic bags around them and store them in a cool, dry place.

### STEP 1
Set the twisted stems in the plaster and cover the top with stones; the stems may need support while the plaster dries. When it is set, attach florist foam balls for dried flowers to the stems with strong tape. These should decrease in size toward the top of the stems. Dried flowers are fragile, so handle them with care to prevent them from disintegrating.

### STEP 2
Using prewired flowerheads, cover each ball completely. Use glue only for lightweight heads.

### STEP 3
Repeat the process with all the foam balls. You can make each one different, or all of them the same, but the design will be stronger if you only use one type of material for each ball.

# MOSS DOG

*You can make a permanent sculpture of any shape, using moist sphagnum moss to stuff and cover a wire frame. Here we create a dog that could stand among your plants or on guard by the front door.*

## INGREDIENTS
- Strong wire frame
- Chicken wire
- Moss
- Fishing line
- Scissors
- Wire cutters

### STEP 1
Make the base frame from heavy duty wire and cover it roughly with chicken wire (*see* Making Frames pp.14-19). Then fill the frame with moss to create the shape, packing it down firmly. For fine details, bind the moss onto the shape with fishing line.

### STEP 3

Trim the moss to create a smooth, finished design.

### AFTERCARE

This will dry out naturally and lighten in color, but needs no aftercare. It will be effective placed on its own or in among various plants as a natural sculpture.

### STEP 2

Cover the moss and wire base with another layer of moss bound on with fishing line; be careful that it doesn't show.

# FLOWERING DISPLAYS

*These colorful designs can be either permanent displays,
using flowering plants, or can be created for a special occasion, using
cut flowers in season.*

### AMARYLLIS TREE

You can create this effect with
flowering bulbs of *Hippeastrum*
(amaryllis) planted in suitable potting
soil and covered with stones, or by
placing the stems of cut flowers in
florist foam, and once again covering
the base with decorative stones. The
silver wire, spiralling around the stems,
is added for decorative effect.

### PHALAENOPSIS SCULPTURE

Place a plant which will flower for
several weeks in a decorative container,
or push cut stems of the orchid into
wet florist foam. Add twisted stems of
willow or witch hazel for dramatic
effect.

### DAISY TREE

This can be a simple standard tree of
*Argyranthemum frutescens*
(marguerite) decorated for a wedding
or, as we have made here, a slightly
more elaborate version using mixed
florists' chrysanthemums and foliage
inserted into wet florist foam.

# GROUPED DISPLAYS

*Displays gain added impact from being grouped together and it affords
an opportunity to show your creative flair for using plants and flowers
to decorate your home.*

### SPRING BULBS

Create a miniature woodland to
enjoy indoors by planting several
groups of the same type of *Narcissus*
(daffodil) in an attractive container
and then adding some twigs of
*Cornus* (dogwood).

### MINIATURE TOPIARY

Growing and preserved topiaries
in varying shapes and sizes make
an interesting group. This is a
pleasing decoration for a wide,
light windowsill, out of the sun, a
shelf or a low table.

### CACTUS COLLECTION

Rather than having several little pots
of cacti, you can produce a desert
scene by planting them together in a
large, shallow bowl. Add sand, and
some broken pieces of terracotta pot
for a finishing touch.

# DIRECTORY OF PLANTS

The list of living plants and dried materials in the Directory is by no means exhaustive, but it gives a selection of the range of subjects that can be used for quick and easy indoor topiary; your choice is governed by the type of sculpture you wish to create. The plants in the Living Directory are listed alphabetically by their scientific names. All the information you need about them is contained under the different headings. The flexible nature of topiary means that you will not be restricted by your local climate to the usual range of plants that you can grow in the open garden, but can choose from many more tender plants that can be grown in containers and brought indoors. The pictures (left), from this chapter, illustrate brilliant amaryllis which can be twined with soft silver thread to make a flowering display; preserved beech leaves, snipped from the branch and ready for pinning onto florist foam; loose heads of Helichrysum bracteatum (everlasting, strawflower), which can either be wired into bunches or stuck singly onto florist foam; and ivy, ideal for trailing around a shape.

# Directory of Living Plants

This directory of fresh materials gives you more specific information about the plants used in this book—where possible, alternatives have been suggested that would also be suitable for these projects and your own designs.

We have identified the plants by their botanical names: the way groups of plants and particular species are recognized internationally. We have also given common names—these can vary between countries.

Under the heading **Uses** we give suggestions for the style of topiary most suited to that type of plant. **Characteristics** explains the features and habits of the plant; this is especially helpful for plants that can only spend a short time indoors. **Training** contains advice that will help you create the final sculpture and maintain your chosen shape. **Cultivation** explains the ways in which you can propagate new plants to replace your specimens or to increase their number. **Maturity** shows you how long it takes for a plant to reach maturity; that is, whether it is slow- or quick-growing. **Permanence** gives an indication as to how long a plant will last given the appropriate care.

The symbols give a quick visual reference to the needs of each plant—the level of care, the temperature, the type of light, the flowering period, and if the plant can go outdoors.

## ARGYRANTHEMUM
### MARGUERITE

**Uses**  Flowering standards.

**Characteristics**  Formerly listed under Chrysanthemum, these evergreen, bushy, woody-stemmed plants have single or double or daisy-like flowers in white, pink or yellow. The green to gray-green or silver-blue foliage is divided and in some varieties reduced to fine thread-like leaflets. One of the best varieties for standards is *Argyranthemum frutescens* with white, single flowers and a bright yellow central disk. Another good choice is the sugar-pink 'Vancouver' with green foliage. Some dwarf types could be used to make mini-standards.

**Training**  Pinch out shoot tips to encourage the formation of a bushy, dense head, once the stem has been trained to the desire height.

**Cultivation**  Grow in well-drained, soil-based potting soil and provide pink and yellow varieties with some shade. Propagate by softwood cuttings taken in early fall. Keep the soil moist at all times.

**Maturity**  Grows quite quickly.

**Permanence**  Fairly long-lasting, given proper care.

Level of care - low to medium

40°F – 75°F

Bright, full sun, some shade for colored varieties

Late spring to early fall

Patio

## BUXUS

BOXWOOD

Level of care - medium

Average to below average, cool in winter 40°F - 70°F

Bright, with some direct sunlight

Patio

**Uses**  Clipped topiary and standards.
**Characteristics**  Although ideally an outdoor shrub, boxwood will tolerate indoor temperatures for short periods. It produces densely-packed, small, shiny leaves on woody stems which, when trimmed, thicken out to produce good shapes for topiary. *Buxus sempervirens* and *Buxus microphylla* are most suitable for small topiary. Boxwood is tolerant of most temperatures but must have good light all year to stop the leaves turning yellow. If possible, place the plant outside in summer. Water thoroughly, but let the potting soil dry out before watering again, to prevent it becoming waterlogged.
**Training**  Needs pruning—to prevent cut marks on the leaves, pinch off new growth.
**Cultivation**  Use soil-based potting soil and provide good drainage. Propagate by semi-hard shoot cuttings in late summer. Use hormone rooting powder and put the cuttings in a cool place.
**Maturity**  A slow-growing plant.
**Permanence**  A long-lasting shrub, but needs regular maintenance.

## CACTUS SPP. (*see* page 104)

## CHAMAECYPARIS (*see* page 106)

## CHLOROPHYTUM COMOSUM

SPIDER PLANT

**Uses**  Decorative textured leaves.
**Characteristics**  A very popular plant that is quick-growing and will survive in most conditions from warm rooms to cold hallways. It can't really be trained, but its leaves arch from a central core and are ideal for hanging arrangements. It does best in a light location, which helps to maintain the vivid green and white stripes in the long, grass-like leaves. It will tolerate dry conditions but prefers a moist atmosphere, such as that found in a bathroom. Regular misting will help the plant to thrive.
**Cultivation**  Produces small plantlets on extended stems. These can be removed and rooted very easily to start new plants, so this plant constantly regenerates itself. Repot in spring if necessary.
**Maturity**  Very quick-growing and produces new plants readily.
**Permanence**  A well-cared for plant will last for many years.

Level of care - low

45°F - 70°F

Good light all the year round, but avoid direct sunlight

# CACTUS SPP.

### CACTUS

Level of care -
low

50°F - 70°F

A very sunny
spot, especially
in winter

**Uses** Sculptural ornamental plants.

**Characteristics** Cacti form a vast family of mainly desert plants, and are ideal if plants are likely to be neglected for long periods. They have a tough outer skin, covered with either spines or hairs, which helps them to retain water but can make them difficult to handle. They require warm conditions in spring and summer but cool temperatures during winter. Water sparingly only when the potting soil has almost completely dried out. During fall and winter they need very little water. After 3–4 years, some cacti produce bright, exotic flowers, which are borne on the new growth. Do not mist the plants, and if possible give them a spell outdoors in summer.

**Training** No special support is needed.

**Cultivation** Take stem cuttings, but these rot easily, so allow the cuttings or offshoots to dry out for a few days before potting in moist, peat-based potting soil.

**Maturity** Slow-growing; although even the small specimens are interesting.

**Permanence** Very long-lasting and some can grow into large plants.

### TRICHOCEREUS SPP.

These cacti tend to have slender stems with strong spines. Some species grow quite large, but most reach only about 1½ feet (45 cm) in height and have a sprawling habit. Red, white or yellow flowers are produced, at night or during the day according to species.

### CEREUS PERUVIANUS

A columnar, branching species that in nature can grow to 15 feet (4.5 m), but will remain smaller in a pot. It makes an interesting-looking specimen and when larger, approx. 6 ft (1.8 m), will produce white flowers at night.

### CEREUS PERUVIANUS 'MONSTROSUS'

'Monstrose' growth is like 'cristate' growth in that it is caused by a genetic fault or damage to the growing point— in this case, the growth is stunted and often results in a knobbly-shaped plant.

## OPUNTIA SUBULATA

Another cactus that in nature grows very large, but adapts well to life in a container. It is usually branching and sometimes in summer has rare, reddish flowers during the day.

## MAMMILLARIA 'CRISTATE'

The genus, Mammillaria, has stems which are usually cylindrical or globular in shape. Silky, white hairs arise from areoles on the stem covering the plant; giving it a whitish appearance. In this case, a "cristate" form can be seen where the growing tip flattens and "fans" out—this is caused either by mutation of the stems or damage to the growing point.

## MAMMILLARIA ELONGATA

The spines on this cactus can range in color from yellow to brown, and together with its contorted form, make it a colorful, unusual plant.

## MAMMILLARIA BOMBYCINA

This cactus produces clusters of slightly cylindrical heads which grow to about 8 inches (20 cm) high. In summer, it bears purplish-brown flowers which bloom during the day.

## EUPHORBIA ELEGANS

This plant is a succulent—the plant group to which cacti belong. All succulent plants have evolved to cope with the stresses of water shortage, and this euphorbia is an example of the divergence of evolution. Take care if you damage the stems of such plants; the white liquid they leak is highly poisonous and can cause blindness.

## CLEISTOCACTUS SPP.

Cacti of this genus are columnar in form and are covered in long, hairy spines, which give the stems a whitish appearance. Mainly red flowers appear in summer, during the day or at night according to the species.

# CHAMAECYPARIS

## FALSE CYPRESS

Level of care – low

Cool to average warmth 45°F - 70°F

Bright light but avoid direct sunlight

Patio

**Uses** Traditional clipped shapes and standards.

**Characteristics** Upright-growing conifers with dense foliage are ideal for sculptural topiaries that require little maintenance. Like most conifers, the *Chamaecyparis* is scented, evergreen, and fully hardy, and may be used for indoor decoration for short periods. However, because of space limitations, not all homes are suitable for conifers; the plants also require cool conditions and a light location such as a balcony, or porch. However, if clipped and watered regularly, the foliage should not suffer when the plant is kept inside for short periods. Put it outdoors for the summer if possible.

**Training** Younger plants are easier to train into shape, since older plants do not produce sufficient new growth to cover any bare areas.

**Cultivation** Use soil-based potting soil with good drainage to prevent the plant from becoming waterlogged. Repot every 2 years to encourage new growth. Propagate in the spring by taking stem cuttings from the current year's growth.

**Maturity** Slow-growing, but can be trimmed to produce shapes after about 3 years.

**Permanence** Can grow into a very large tree, depending on the variety. Not all are suitable for indoor decoration.

### CHAMAECYPARIS LAWSONIANA 'PEMBURY BLUE' (LAWSON CYPRESS)

A conical tree with pendulous sprays of bright blue-gray foliage, this cypress is quite difficult to train because it is slow-growing. It reaches 7 feet (2.1 m) in 10 years.

### CHAMAECYPARIS LAWSONIANA 'GREYSWOOD FEATHER' (LAWSON CYPRESS)

This tree has a columnar habit and dark green, feathery foliage. It will grow to 5 feet (1.5 m) in 10 years.

### CHAMAECYPARIS PISIFERA 'BOULEVARD' (SAWARA CYPRESS)

This is a wide-spreading conifer with small clusters of silver-blue foliage. It will reach 5 feet (1.5 m) in 10 years.

### CHAMAECYPARIS LAWSONIANA 'ELWOODII' (LAWSON CYPRESS)

An erect tree, with feathery, gray-green foliage, which forms a compact column. This dwarf form grows slowly, reaching 6 feet (1.8 m) in 10 years.

# FICUS BENJAMINA

## WEEPING FIG

# FICUS PUMILA

## CREEPING FIG

**Uses**  Standard topiary.

**Characteristics**  Weeping figs are part of a large group of plants with graceful, simple central stems and they can easily be clipped to form standard topiaries. They have different leaf shapes and types of variegated markings. This is a good plant for modern homes because it is tolerant of central heating. However, it doesn't like change once it has established itself and may lose leaves if left in a draft. Water carefully, allowing the potting soil to dry out between waterings; mist the plant in summer.

**Training**  Once you have pruned the tree to the required shape, regular clipping or pinching off of the new growth is required to encourage the flower branches to thicken and produce new leaf growth.

**Cultivation**  Propagate from stem cuttings in summer, using hormone rooting powder. Plant in good potting soil and feed the plant during the period of growth.

**Maturity**  Can be pruned after 1 year, but it will take 3–4 years to establish the shape.

**Permanence**  Should last for years and can grow to 6 feet (1.8 m) if well cared for.

**Uses**  Training over moss-covered frames.

**Characteristics**  One of a diverse group of plants, this is an excellent creeper which clings to any damp surface. It puts down roots as it grows, so is ideal for moss-covered shapes and poles. The main requirement with this plant is that it is kept moist at all times and it will soon suffer if left dry. This can make it difficult to keep, but if you avoid direct sunlight and keep it in a humid atmosphere, it will grow quickly. Misting will keep the plant healthy if it is kept in dry conditions. A vigorous climber; in ideal conditions it can cover an area 2 foot square (18.5 square cm).

**Training**  As new shoots develop, pin them into the moss to create the shape. Pinch off the tips to thicken the plant.

**Cultivation**  Grow in well-drained peat-based potting soil. Propagate by taking tip cuttings in spring. Dip the base of the cuttings in hormone rooting powder and place them in a pot with a plastic bag over the top to retain moisture. Give the cuttings some heat from below, if possible.

**Maturity**  Quick-growing, but will become leggy if not trimmed.

**Permanence**  A difficult plant to keep going.

Level of care - medium

55°F - 70°F

Bright spot to retain variegated markings

Level of care - medium to high

55°F - 70°F

Can stand in bright light but will dry out in direct sunlight

## FITTONIA VERSCHAFFELTII 'NANA'

### SNAKESKIN PLANT

Level of care—
medium to high

50°F – 75°F

Needs some
shade from
direct sunlight

**Uses**  Decorative foliage for moss-filled frames.

**Characteristics**  An attractive creeper with soft leaves that is good as ground cover. This small-leaved type is much more tolerant of central heating, so it doesn't need the special growing conditions that larger Fittonias do. Keep the potting soil moist but don't let it get waterlogged, especially in winter. Mist the plant frequently and place out of direct sunlight to prevent the edges of the leaves from turning brown.

**Training**  Pin new shoots into the moss base as they develop. Cut back straggly shoots and any flower stems that develop.

**Cultivation**  Use soil-based potting soil that has good moisture-retaining qualities. In spring, propagate by dividing the plant or by separating rooted offsets from around the edge of the plant and potting them individually.

**Maturity**  Quick-growing, but needs dividing; otherwise it will become straggly.

**Permanence**  Not an easy plant to keep going, but if kept in warm conditions and divided from time to time, you should have constant growth.

## GLORIOSA ROTHSCHILDIANA

### GLORY LILY

Level of care –
high

50°F – 75°F

Bright position,
but shade from
direct sunlight

Midsummer

**Uses**  Trailing around a frame.

**Characteristics**  In summer, this exotic climber produces large red and yellow flowers with turned-back petals. The stems need support since they are very weak and the weight of the flowers will snap them. The plant climbs by means of tendrils that grow from the leaf tips, and once the plant is established it is difficult to untangle the tendrils without damaging them. It needs a warm, well-lit position during flowering. Water well in the growing period and mist occasionally to keep the humidity high.

**Training**  If not controlled early on, this plant will establish its own form, which is then difficult to alter. Support the stems as they develop and tie them into the frame as they grow.

**Cultivation**  Glory lilies are best grown from a tuber so that the growth can be controlled from the time it appears. When the plant dies back, store the tuber in a safe place: then the tuber can be divided and replanted the following spring.

**Maturity**  Quick-growing.

**Permanence**  Will die back each season but grow again if replanted after storage.

## HEDERA SPP.

### IVY

Level of care - low

45° F - 60° F

Bright light in winter, no direct sunlight in summer

Patio

**Uses** Training on frames or moss-covered shapes.

**Characteristics** A large group of versatile trailing plants which adapt to most conditions, but are not as easy to keep as is often thought. Most are suitable for topiary, but the smaller-leaved varieties are easiest to work with. Ivies come in many different leaf shapes, color variations, and forms, but all prefer cool conditions and don't really like the dry air of centrally heated rooms. Misting will help to prevent the edges of leaves turning brown due to drying out. Water ivies regularly, allowing the surface of the soil to dry out between waterings; give less water in winter but do not let the soil dry out completely.

**Training** These plants often don't even need to be tied into shape—you just wind the new growth around the frame and the stems will develop around the shape. Ivies climb and branch out freely and cover bare areas quickly.

**Cultivation** The quickest way to establish a new plant is to cut a single side shoot with roots on it from the main plant and pot it. Stem cuttings dipped in hormone rooting powder will also take without any trouble.

**Maturity** Quick-growing and will cover almost any area or object.

**Permanence** Plants becomes a bit woody after a few years, so add in new growth periodically.

**HEDERA HELIX 'SILVER EMERALD'**
This variety has silvery leaves, with all three lobes pointing forward. It is a vigorous grower.

**HEDERA HELIX 'GOLDSTERN'**
This ivy has little lime-green, arrow-shaped leaves with a splash of dark green in the center.

### HEDERA HELIX 'NEILSON'
A vigorous grower with small, dark green, pointed leaves.

### HEDERA HELIX 'SILVER KING'
The variegated, arrow-shaped leaves of this ivy have five lobes, the central one being much larger than the others.

### HEDERA ALGERIENSIS 'STAUSS'
This ivy has mid-green, heart-shaped leaves extending into a three-pointed lobe, and a red stem.

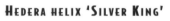

### HEDERA HELIX 'ATROPURPUREA'
(PURPLE-LEAVED IVY)
This plant has dark-green, heart-shaped leaves that turn purple in winter.

## HELXINE SOLEIROLII

MIND-YOUR-OWN-BUSINESS, BABY'S TEARS

## HIPPEASTRUM HYBRIDA

AMARYLLIS

Level of care -
medium to high

45°F - 70°F

Bright light but
avoid direct
sunlight

Patio

**Uses**  Covering moss-filled frames and potting soil.

**Characteristics**  The rapid growth and mat-forming habit of this plant, also known as *Soleirolia soleirolii*, make it ideal for covering large areas. It has a profusion of tiny round leaves (those of *Helxine argentea* are silvery green) which, although delicate-looking, survive in most temperatures. When grown inside, it needs a bright location, shaded from direct sunlight.

**Training**  Little maintenance is needed, but trim the plant if it becomes straggly.

**Cultivation**  Use good water-retentive potting soil to stop the roots drying out, with plenty of drainage material to prevent it from becoming waterlogged. In summer, keep the soil damp but do not overwater; give less water in winter. Keep the plant cool and mist it regularly to maintain humidity. Propagate by pulling small rooted clumps from the mother plant and replanting them in fresh, moist potting soil.

**Maturity**  Quick-growing, can cover 1 foot square (9 cm square) and produce large mounds.

**Permanence**  New plants can be established very easily, so discard old plants when they look patchy or straggly.

**Uses**  Flowering bulb.

**Characteristics**  Flamboyant plant grown mainly for indoor decoration. A single stem is produced with little foliage. In late fall, several trumpet-shaped flowers are produced at the top of the stem. Flower colors are usually plain red, pink, orange and white, but some attractive striped varieties exist. The flowers persist for many weeks.

**Training**  The stem may need support because of the weight of the flowerhead.

**Cultivation**  Raise from seed in spring or propagate from offshoots of the main bulb in fall. Water well during the period of active growth. When the leaves die back, store the bulb in slightly damp peat moss and repot it the following season.

**Maturity**  Reaches full size each season.

**Permanence**  If stored and rested after flowering is finished, the bulb will last for several years.

Level of care -
medium to high

Cool to medium
warm
45°F - 65°F

Bright position
with some shade

Late fall to early
spring

## HYPOESTES PHYLLOSTACHYA

POLKA DOT PLANT

Level of care - low

50°F - 70°F

Bright light and some direct sunlight to keep colors vivid

**Uses** Decorative leaves in moss or potting-soil shapes.

**Characteristics** These plants are grown for their spotted leaves, which come in a variety of colors from deep pink to pale green and white. The markings are particularly vivid when the plant is kept in bright light; in shade, they will revert to plain green. The insignificant flowers detract from the foliage and should be pinched off. Keep the potting soil constantly moist during the growing season and mist the leaves frequently to prevent the plant from drying out.

**Training** Pinch off the new growth to encourage the plant to fill out and to keep it compact.

**Cultivation** Can be grown from seed in spring or from stem cuttings in the summer. If started under plastic, they will take more quickly. Repot every spring.

**Maturity** Quick-growing, but can become leggy and unattractive.

**Permanence** Needs replacing after a few seasons.

## JASMINUM POLYANTHUM

PINK JASMINE

**Uses** Training over frames.

**Characteristics** Although known as pink jasmine, the sweetly-scented flowers are mainly white. The small, pointed, dark green leaves grow on long, trailing stems. These plants are mainly bought in flower to bring color and scent into the home in winter and spring. Once they have finished flowering, the shoots can grow rapidly—and quickly get out of shape—so regular trimming or training is required. This plant will benefit from being placed outside during the summer. Do not let it dry out in warm conditions and mist the leaves regularly.

**Training** Wind new growth around the frame and secure it with wire ties if necessary.

**Cultivation** Grow in soil-based potting soil and propagate by taking stem cuttings in the spring or heel cuttings in summer. Use hormone rooting powder and keep the cuttings in a warm place until they have developed good root systems.

**Maturity** Quick-growing once established.

**Permanence** Should flower every year.

Level of care - low

Average warmth 45°F - 75°F

Bright with some direct sunlight

Midwinter to spring

Patio

## LAURUS NOBILIS

SWEET BAY

Level of care -
low

45°F - 55°F

Bright and some
direct sunlight
to avoid
yellowing leaves

Patio

**Uses**  Standards, and traditional topiary shapes.

**Characteristics**  This plant produces aromatic leaves used in cooking and for drying. Its bushy nature and large leaves make it ideal for simple, topiary shapes. In spring, it produces small, insignificant flowers, which are followed by small, dark fruits. It is a relatively quick-growing shrub that can grow 3 feet tall (90 cm) in 3 years. Bay needs a sunny spot and fresh air where possible.

**Training**  This is an easy plant to shape; use pruning shears to clip branches but not the leaves, since this will make unsightly marks on them. The plant may need clipping twice a year to maintain a good shape.

**Cultivation**  A soil-based potting soil with good drainage is important. Do not overwater, especially in winter. Misting will help to keep the bay healthy if it is kept for long periods inside. Turn the plant around from time to time for even growth. Take stem cuttings in spring or fall.

**Maturity**  The plant will take 3–4 years to achieve a mature shape.

**Permanence**  A long-lasting shrub that can be planted outdoors if it grows too big.

## LEUCOBRYUM GLAUCUM

BUN MOSS

**Uses**  Covering frames filled with potting soil or moss.

**Characteristics**  Bun moss forms the blue-gray cushions of moss found in woodlands with acid soil, or in bogs. It should not be removed from wild woodlands. It can be used fresh or dried out, but even if kept dry, it will start to grow again when it is wetted. This moss is used mainly for its decorative qualities—to cover bare potting soil and moss-covered frames—but it also helps to retain moisture. It must be kept damp to preserve its color.

**Training**  Wires can be used to secure the bun moss onto moss-filled frames; otherwise it needs no special attention.

**Permanence**  Can be reused several times, even if it has dried out.

Level of care -
low

40°F - 60°F

Some bright
light is needed
to retain color

Patio

## LIGUSTRUM OVALIFOLIUM

PRIVET

**Uses**  Clipped topiary shapes.

**Characteristics**  This shrub is not ideal as a permanent feature indoors, but it can successfully be brought in for short periods. It is generally used as a hedging plant, but because of its rapid, dense regrowth and pliable stems it makes a good base for topiary. Golden privet, *Ligustrum ovalifolium* 'Aureum', has small, oval, yellow leaves and little, white flowers in midsummer, which are followed by black berries in fall. If the leaves start to drop, move the plant to a cooler location.

**Training**  Clip as traditional topiary in mid-spring and tie back new growth when necessary.

**Cultivation**  Use any well-drained potting soil. Propagate by softwood cuttings in late spring or hardwood cuttings in winter.

**Maturity**  Although the plant is quick-growing, topiary shapes will take 2–3 years to develop.

**Permanence**  Will continue to thrive for many years and can be placed outside permanently if it becomes too large.

Level of care - medium to high

40°F - 60°F

Bright position with some shade

Midsummer

Patio

## NARCISSUS SPP.

DAFFODIL

**Uses**  Flowering bulbs.

**Characteristics**  An ideal plant for indoor color and fragrance, producing flowers in winter and spring. Plant in early fall and the flowers will appear from midwinter through to spring. The flowers may be single, double or multi-headed and come in shades of yellow, cream, and white.

**Training**  May need some support as the flowers develop, since they can make the plant top heavy.

**Cultivation**  Keep in a cool place and water regularly but sparingly. Narcissus bulbs can be stored when the foliage dies down after flowering. They will increase naturally by the production of offsets and clumps, and can be divided every 2–3 years to produce new plants.

**Maturity**  Will reach full-size each season.

**Permanence**  The bulbs can be used for many years indoors and can then be planted outside.

Level of care - medium

Cool

Bright and will tolerate full winter sun

Winter through to spring

Patio

## NERTERA GRANADENSIS

### BEAD PLANT

## PASSIFLORA CAERULEA

### PASSION FLOWER

Level of care - medium to high

40°F - 50°F

Bright with some direct sunlight

Patio

**Uses** In frames filled with moss or potting soil.

**Characteristics** The bead plant produces a mass of small green leaves in a carpet that provides good cover for displays. Insignificant flowers in the spring are followed by orange bead-like berries in late summer that will often last into the winter. When the plant is not covered with berries, it resembles *Helxine soleirolii*, but it is much less vigorous and hardy and requires regular watering and misting to keep it constantly moist. It also likes fresh air and bright light. Plants can be kept outside in summer and brought inside when the berries appear.

**Training** The plant will creep slowly over the surface of the moss or potting soil, but needs no real training.

**Cultivation** Divide mature plants when the berries die off and plant the divisions in fresh, well-drained potting soil. Nertera will tolerate a shady spot outside in summer.

**Maturity** Slow-growing.

**Permanence** Usually discarded after one season, but plants can be kept going if you look after them.

**Uses** Training around frames.

**Characteristics** A quick-growing climber with glossy leaves. The parts of the unusual flowers are said to represent different aspects of the Crucifixion of Christ. The flowers are short-lived but appear in succession all summer. Passionflower can be trained up a frame but will need regular attention to keep in shape. It needs plenty of water in summer and must not be allowed to dry out. It is most suitable for a very light situation, such as a sunroom, but needs some shade in high summer.

**Training** If bought as a mature plant, passionflower is quite difficult to untangle because of the complex structure of the tendrils. It is better to start with a young plant and train it as it grows.

**Cultivation** Use well-drained, soil-based potting soil. Propagate in spring by sowing seed in a heated propagator, or by taking stem cuttings in summer and providing bottom heat to encourage rapid growth. Repot mature plants every spring.

**Maturity** Quick-growing; cut it back to prevent it from smothering other plants.

**Permanence** Will die back and re-establish itself every year. Can be placed outside if protected from winter frosts.

Level of care - medium

40°F - 75°F

Bright position with some shade

Early to late summer

Patio

## PHALAENOPSIS HYBRIDS

### MOTH ORCHID

**Uses**  Ornamental flowering plant.
**Characteristics**  Very popular because of its simple, stunning, flat, white flowers borne on arching stems, this orchid is not as difficult to look after as is often thought. Needs a light location with some shade in summer, and a steady warm temperature with high humidity, so a greenhouse or heated sunroom is ideal. Moth orchids have no specific flowering period and can be bought in bloom all the year round. Keep the potting soil damp but not wet in the growing period, and just moist during the winter rest period. New flower stems grow as old ones die back. Needs to be fed regularly with special orchid fertilizer.
**Training**  The stems are long and thin and many large flowers are produced, so always support the stem as it develops.
**Cultivation**  The plant must be grown in special fibrous orchid potting soil, and should be repotted every other year. Propagation is difficult, but the plant can be divided at the end of the rest period.
**Maturity**  Slow-growing initially.
**Permanence**  Will flower for months on end if temperature and conditions are right.

Level of care - high

50°F – 80F

Bright in winter, shaded in summer

All year round

## PILEA CADIEREI

### ALUMINUM PLANT

**Uses**  Decorative leaf cover on moss and potting soil frames.
**Characteristics**  One of a group of low-growing, bushy, variegated plants. Pilea is relatively easy to grow and will quickly form a carpet of small, textured leaves. This variety has silvery patches on the upper leaf surface, which explains its common name. These plants suffer in the cold, so should be taken off a windowsill on cold nights and be kept out of drafts. Water well with lukewarm water during the growing season, but let the potting soil dry out slightly between waterings.
**Training**  Pinch off stem tips to encourage the plant to remain bushy, to keep it low-growing, and prevent it becoming leggy.
**Cultivation**  These plants tend to get straggly, so it is better to start new plants from stem cuttings each season. These will root quickly if you use hormone rooting powder, and will soon mature to good-sized plants easily.
**Maturity**  Grows to full-size in one season.
**Permanence**  Needs to be replaced regularly.

Level of care - low

45°f – 70°F

Bright with some shade, protect from direct sunlight

## RHOICISSUS RHOMBOIDEA

GRAPE IVY

## ROSMARINUS OFFICINALIS

ROSEMARY

Level of care - low

40°F - 50°F

Bright with some shade, protect from direct sunlight

**Uses**  Climbing and training around frames.

**Characteristics**  Also known as *Cissus rhombifolia*. The common name, grape ivy, is misleading, since the plant is more like a vine in appearance. It is quick-growing and produces dark, glossy leaves with small bunches of dark fruits similar to bunches of grapes. It is a tolerant house plant suitable for most conditions and can grow to some 10 feet (3 m). Do not let the soil dry out, especially in the summer, and mist the leaves in dry conditions.

**Training**  This plant will grow up a support or down in a hanging arrangement, but will need to be tied in since it is a vigorous grower and may not grow in the required direction. But, do not tie the stems in too tightly, since this can cause damage and restrict growth.

**Cultivation**  Propagate by means of softwood cuttings in spring or summer.

**Maturity**  Very quick-growing.

**Permanence**  Long-lasting, but the plant may need dividing and repotting to keep it healthy.

**Uses**  Clipped shapes, covered frames and standards.

**Characteristics**  Rosemary is an evergreen shrub grown for its attractive and aromatic dark gray-green needles, which are used in cooking and in decoration. It produces small blue flowers mainly in spring. 'Miss Jessop's Upright' is a strongly vertical variety particularly suitable for topiary. If kept inside, set the plant in a light place, such as a windowsill and turn it regularly to produce even growth. Do not overwater.

**Training**  If using a wire frame, tie in the new shoots to encourage growth in the right direction rather than try to bend the stems of established plants. Pinch out tips to encourage the lower growth to thicken. Clip in spring, after flowering, using scissors or pruning shears. To prevent stems becoming woody, remove one-third of the old growth at this time.

**Cultivation**  Grow in well-drained, gritty potting soil. Propagate in late summer from heel cuttings, stripped of the lower bark, then dipped in hormone rooting powder.

**Maturity**  Grows quickly and will soon re-establish itself after clipping.

**Permanence**  Long-lasting, but must be cut back hard every few years.

Level of care - medium

40°F - 60°F

Full sun

Late spring to early summer

Patio

## STEPHANOTIS FLORIBUNDA

STEPHANOTIS

### VIBURNUM TINUS

LAURUSTINUS

**Uses**  Training around frames.
**Characteristics**  A vigorous climber with glossy, broad leaves and strong stems, it will need supporting as it can grow very big. It is best known for its waxy, heavily scented flowers produced in summer or, when forced, much later in the year. The long-lasting flowers are used for bridal work. Stephanotis can be a very temperamental plant, and hates sudden changes of temperature. It must be kept cool during winter, and the potting soil should be allowed to dry out slightly between waterings. Mist during summer.
**Training**  If the stems are wound around each other as they grow they will support each other and provide an even distribution of flowers.
**Cultivation**  Grow in a peat- or soil-based potting soil. Propagate by taking cuttings from nonflowering stems in summer. Use hormone rooting powder and provide bottom heat, preferably in a propagator.
**Maturity**  The plant is slow-growing and may take several seasons to flower.
**Permanence**  Can be kept and maintained for several years.

**THUJA OCCIDENTALIS**  (*see* page 120)

**Uses**  Standard and topiary shapes.
**Characteristics**  An evergreen shrub mainly grown outside, but it will be quite happy in a light, cool location in the home. It often blooms twice a year, producing small, scented white flowers. It has dark green, dense foliage that can be clipped into standard or other shapes. Water well in the growing season and remember that pot-grown specimens will dry out quickly. Repot in spring if necessary, and set the plant outside during the summer.
**Training**  Remove foliage from stems to create standards and clip new growth often to encourage bushiness and prevent the plant from becoming leggy.
**Cultivation**  Grow in well-drained, soil-based potting soil. Cover the soil with stones or moss to help retain moisture. Propagate by softwood cuttings in summer, using hormone rooting powder and providing bottom heat to start with.
**Maturity**  This is a quick-growing shrub, which will reach maturity in 2–3 years.
**Permanence**  Long-lasting, and can be brought into the house year after year.

Level of care - high

45°F – 75°F

Bright spot out of direct sunlight

Early summer to mid-fall

Level of care - low to medium

Cool to below average, cool in winter

Bright light with some shade during summer

Late fall to late spring

Patio

# THUJA OCCIDENTALIS

## WHITE CEDAR

Level of care -
low

Cool to average
warmth
45°F - 70°F

Bright light but
avoid direct
sunlight

Patio

**Uses** Traditional clipped shapes and standards.

**Characteristics** Dense, fast-growing foliage is ideal for sculptural topiaries that require little maintenance. This conifer is often highly aromatic and comes in a wide variety of green, yellow, and gray shades. Because of their size, not all homes are suitable for conifers; the plants also require cool conditions and a light location. However, if clipped and watered regularly, the foliage should not suffer when the plant is kept inside for short periods. Put it outdoors for the summer if possible.

**Training** Younger plants are easier to train into shape, since older plants do not produce sufficient new growth to cover any bare areas.

**Cultivation** Use soil-based potting soil with good drainage to prevent the plant becoming waterlogged. Repot every 2 years to encourage new growth. Propagate in the spring by taking stem cuttings from the current year's growth.

**Maturity** Slow-growing, but can be trimmed to produce shapes after about 3 years.

**Permanence** Can grow into a very large tree, depending on the variety. Not all are suitable for indoor decoration.

## THUJA OCCIDENTALIS 'SMARAGD'

This slow-growing variety is conical in shape, with neat, erect rows of bright green leaves. It will reach 6–7 feet (1.8–2.1 m) in height in 10 years.

## THUJA OCCIDENTALIS 'SUNKIST'

This very ornamental, conical-shaped tree keeps its gold color all the year round. It is a very slow-growing dwarf form that reaches only 3 feet (90 cm) in 10 years.

## THUJA OCCIDENTALIS 'ERICOIDES'

A low-growing bushy plant, with fine neeedle-like leaves that turn reddish purple in winter. It grows very slowly and will reach 3 feet (90 cm) in 10 years.

## THUJA OCCIDENTALIS 'RHEINGOLD'

The yellow-orange foliage of this dwarf form turns bronze in winter. The tree grows to only 3 feet (90 cm) in height in 10 years.

# Directory of Preserved & Dried Plants

*Dried and preserved flowers and foliage have been popular since the nineteenth century, when the idea of being able to keep flowers in the home long after their normal life span first became popular. They are still used for interior decoration and have many advantages. They are particularly useful in low-light areas, where fresh flowers and plants would not survive. Preserved materials are also popular because they do not require constant maintenance. However, many people dislike them because they can collect dust and will deteriorate in time.*

*The best way to deal with these problems is to use good-quality materials to start with. Place your finished design in a suitable environment that is not too humid or dusty, and in a setting where it will not get knocked over easily. You might consider displaying your dried arrangements for only a season, perhaps in fall when fresh flowers are not readily available. Afterwards, they can be stored in a cool, dry place and used again the following year.*

### Glycerin-preserved Gaultheria shallon
(SHALLON, SALAL)
Preserved stems of this commercially grown foliage plant, with big, broad leaves, can be used in displays. The leaves alone are good for covering large areas.

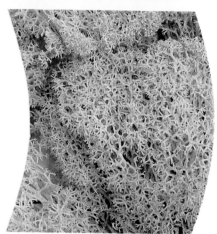

### Glycerin-preserved 'Reindeer' moss
This moss has an interesting texture and comes dyed in a multitude of colors. Because it is preserved, it stays soft to the touch and can easily be pinned or glued to an arrangement.

### Dried Laurus nobilis
(SWEET BAY)
Aromatic bay leaves are dried for use in cooking and in room fresheners. You can dry them yourself, but they may need to be flattened while still fresh to prevent the edges from rolling up.

## CINNAMON STICKS

This is the bark of the tropical tree *Cinnamonum zeylanicum*. It is ground for use as a spice in cooking, and at Christmas it is often tied in bundles and hung on the tree. Cinnamon sticks are available in many sizes: the culinary type is small and expensive.

## DRIED ORANGE SLICES

These orange slices have been dried on a baking tray in a barely warm oven for several hours. Once dried, keep the slices in a dry place, since they can absorb moisture and deteriorate. They can be wired together, strung onto a garland, or glued into arrangements.

## GLYCERIN-PRESERVED HEDERA (IVY)

This mature ivy plant has been preserved and then dyed to give a vivid color. Using such leaves will make your arrangement look far fresher than if you use traditional dried materials, which can be rather subdued in color.

## DRIED CLOVE BUDS

The dried flower buds of the tropical tree *Eugenia aromatica* are used for flavoring food, and clove oil helps to alleviate toothache. Cloves have been popular since the sixteenth century for making pomanders, and, embedded in candles they give off a spicy aroma.

## MIXED NUTS

You can use nuts in many arrangements. Either attach them to other dried materials, or mix them in with cones and leaves. Added to potpourri, they give it an interesting, rougher texture.

## MIXED CONES

Cones come in a wide range of shades and sizes. You can collect or buy a vast array of cones from various types of trees from all over the world. Once dried, they can be used for many different, decorative purposes.

## GLYCERINED ROSES

These roses come in several colors, but only a few sizes. They are commercially preserved with glycerin and are expensive, but you could experiment at home with your own roses. The main advantage they have over dried flowers is that they stay soft, almost damp to the touch, keep their color, and are fairly long-lasting. They do not have stems, so they need to be wired.

## GLYCERIN-PRESERVED FAGUS SYLVATICA (BEECH)

Beech leaves come in several colors and dye can be added to the glycerin to keep the color consistent. The leaves may otherwise change to many different shades, depending on the state of the plant when it is preserved.

## STAR ANISE (ANISEED)

The seed pod of the anise plant is not only attractive, but also has a wonderful scent. It is used for flavoring cooked dishes, but also has many decorative uses. If you use it to scent a room, put it near a heat source to enhance the fragrance.

## DRIED TRITICUM AESTIVUM (WHEAT)

One of the easiest materials to dry and use, wheat comes in many forms, and can be bleached and dyed to almost any color. It often looks best used on its own.

## DRIED EUCALYPTUS LEAVES

It is easy to dry these yourself by the air-drying method. Stand the stems in a little water, and the leaves will slowly dry out. This is a good way to preserve them, since they will not be damaged, and will keep their natural pale gray coloration.

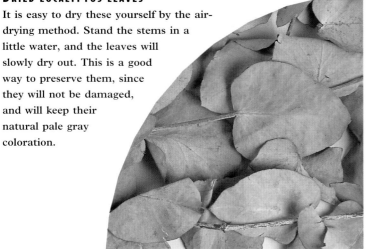

## GLYCERIN-PRESERVED QUERCUS (OAK)

Oak is a traditional foliage of fall, when we tend to display most dried flowers. You should pick all leaves that you want to preserve with glycerin when they show their best fall colors.

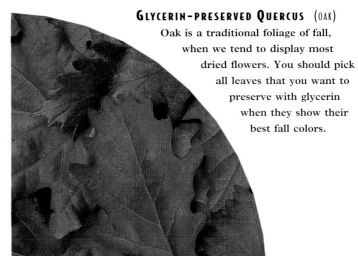

## GLYCERIN-PRESERVED LAVANDULA (LAVENDER)

Lavender is quite easy to grow and dry at home. This lavender has been dyed to enhance the color, which tends to fade quite quickly in strong sunlight. The stems are fine, and wiring them into bunches makes lavender much easier to use.

## DRIED HELICHRYSUM BRACTEATUM (EVERLASTING, STRAWFLOWER)

These inexpensive dried flowers come in colors ranging from white to deep red. Several head shapes exist, and flowers can be bought by the head on their natural stems, which need wiring, since they are brittle. The flowers can also be glued on.

## DRIED FRUITS

You can prepare these items yourself by slow drying methods, but make sure that they are thoroughly dried out, or they will get moldy.

# INDEX

# ACKNOWLEDGEMENTS

*With kind thanks to Pat and her team at C. Best, New Covent Garden Market for her help with all the dried and preserved materials we used, to the Scientific Wire Company for finding just what I needed, and to Avant Garden for supplying the galvanized wire frames used in this book, and to the staff at the Van Hages Garden Centre for their invaluable advice and knowledge about plants.*

*Thanks to Jon for looking after us and putting up with all the mess, to Moira for her patience, to Michelle (Crucial Books, London), who through all her troubles, was always there to help.*

*Special thanks to my invaluable assistant, Jacki (Mum), who did all the preparation, dirty work and clearing up, and last but not least, to Tom, for all he has to put up with, and his special support. The plant and equipment suppliers can be reached at the following addresses:*

*Avant Garden, 77 Ledbury Road, London W11 2AJ, England*
*C. Best, Units P50/55 Flower Market, New Covent Garden Market, Nine Elms, London SW8, England*
*Van Hages Garden Centre, Great Amwell, Ware, Hertfordshire SG12 9RP, England*
*The Scientific Wire Company, 18 Raven Road, London E18 1HW, England*